A Little Faith

A Little Faith

A FATHER'S MIRACLE STORY *of* FAITH, HOPE, LOVE, *and* A MICRO PREEMIE

BOB KRECH

www.beliefbooks.com

Published by Belief Books
PO Box 22701
Hilton Head, SC 29928

Library of Congress Control Number: 2020908163

ISBN 978-1-7349128-0-7 (pbk)
ISBN 978-1-7349128-1-4 (ebook)

Faith is the substance of things hoped for,
the evidence of things not seen.

Hebrews 11:1

DEDICATION AND ACKNOWLEDGMENT

This book is dedicated with much love and many thanks to the nurses and doctors at the Mercer Medical Center NICU, now part of Capital Health at Hopewell. Without them, there would be no story to write or it might have had a very different ending. However, to ensure their privacy, their names have been changed here because it has been so long and I could not possibly track them all down, but they know who they are.

Thanks also to my family and friends for their encouragement, especially my wife, Karen, who was so brave and positive throughout everything. Thanks to the DUTCH NECK SCHOOL family for being there when we needed them, to Kris McBride for being one of the earliest readers and for dispensing good advice and encouragement, to Rosalie Siegel who believed early on, supported, and tried hard to launch the book, to Mary Ann Smith for beautiful design and even more beautiful patience, to Susan VanHecke, who edited this book in every way you can edit a book, to my son, Andrew for his love, positive support, and technical help, and to my daughter, Faith for writing the afterword and being open to all that this endeavor entails.

Finally and foremost, thanks and all glory to God, who is the real author of this miracle.

CONTENTS

FOREWORD

For the last twenty-seven years, on a shelf in my study, there has been a tiny photograph of a tiny baby. The photograph is attached to an index card with these words written in a teacher's hand, *"And I tell you once more that if two of you on earth agree and ask for anything it will be granted to you by my Heavenly Father. For wherever two or three people come together in my name, I am there, right among them!"* (Matthew 18:19-20).

The baby in that photograph is the little Faith of this book and that index card is one of four that were placed in her isolette by her father during the long days that marked her entry into our lives. Unlike our Eastern Orthodox and Roman Catholic siblings, we Presbyterians don't have religious relics--but if we did, that now weathered index card would be a relic of the miracle of which you will read in this beautiful book.

The first time my wife and I met Faith, she was about eight or nine weeks old. Melanie and I followed Faith's mother, Karen into the NICU and there was Bob holding the tiniest baby I'd ever seen. He snuggled the blanket-engulfed infant in his arms and we could hear him saying, "My beautiful girl. My beautiful baby girl." She didn't look beautiful to me. She was so tiny and thin that "fragile" didn't seem to convey the nature of this preemie; and surrounding her more than that seemingly huge blanket, was her father's love. Whatever was to come, this much was clear: Karen and Bob adored this child and whatever was to be asked of them by this truly fragile life, they were responding with unflagging love.

The story that Bob Krech tells is one that I watched from outside. We spoke from time to time. I received reports from Melanie, who worked with Bob. I could not imagine then what the birth of such a child was like for our friends. What we saw was a couple who persevered with a quiet fierceness called love; they didn't give up on Faith, themselves or God. Reading this book has been a revelation for me. More than once, tears have been part of hearing this poignant story of hope. I have also found my own faith in Christ strengthened by being let in to something of Bob and Karen's story. I think it might be the same for you…whatever you believe, I think that this story will be a sign of a Love that is greater than we can imagine. It is the story of Faith and also that Love.

So, if the truth be told, for me and my house, that index card is indeed a relic and this story is the story of a miracle; the miracle of love and prayer and hope….and a little faith.

The Reverend Dr. Gregory C. Faulkner
Senior Pastor
Trinity Presbyterian Church
Cherry Hill, New Jersey

INTRODUCTION

There is a story behind the story. There always is. While my daughter, Faith, was in the hospital struggling to survive her extremely premature birth, I was taking notes just to keep things straight, as there was a lot of information flying at us very quickly. A few years went by and I attempted to assemble the notes and my memories into a book. I've written a lot of books and articles for teachers and kids, but this was the hardest thing I'd ever tried to write. Eventually though, I had a manuscript. This was about 2006. Through one of my editors I found a wonderful agent for the book, Rosalie Siegel. She had been a preemie herself and really appreciated the story.

Rosalie did a great job getting the manuscript to the final table at a number of top-notch Christian publishing houses. The word that came back each time was that they loved the story, loved the writing, but wondered who I was. Did I have a following? Had I been on television? Did I have a blog?

The answer was uniformly no. I was a writer who specialized in books on teaching elementary math. I was not an expert in neonatology or theology, nor was I about to become one. What was there for me to blog about?

The publishers, on hearing this, decided to pass. If I was Charles Barkley writing this book about a preemie birth, they would be on board. But with no built-in fan base to rely on for a potential market, they were unwilling to take a chance.

So I let the book lie. Every year or two, I would take it out again and work on it for a few months. Each time when I thought I was done, I would read it again and feel it was not good enough. It could always be better. It was a slow process and I began to wonder if it would ever actually be finished.

Then 2019 rolled around. Three years earlier my wife, Karen and I had moved south and joined Hilton Head Island Community Church in Hilton Head, South Carolina. As a church we began to read Mark Batterson's *Draw the Circle: The 40 Day Prayer Challenge.* Someone once mentioned to me that when you are reading Psalms in the Bible, just for fun, you should pick out the Psalm number that matches your birthday and that is your psalm. I was born on July 27 (never mind the year!) so for me, it was Psalm 27. I figured let me try the same thing with Batterson's book. I started reading chapter 27. Here's how that chapter starts: "For thirteen years I was a frustrated writer. I had a half-dozen half-finished manuscripts on my computer, but I couldn't seem to finish a book."

What?! Wow! It was like he wrote that chapter for me. He was in that desert for thirteen years. Oh, coincidence that 2019 was the thirteenth year for me on this book too? I think not. I finished the chapter then went back and began reading a chapter a day for forty days. I learned about circling our requests to God in prayer and I began to circle this book in prayer in earnest. Every day.

During the second week of circling the book in prayer, I was at our Wednesday night church Roots meeting. In this group we focus on the sermon from Sunday and go deeper in a small group setting. Someone posed the question, "Have you ever had God break into your life in a miraculous way?" Everyone had a story.

Incredible, moving, poignant stories. I had mine, which was the basis of this book. And it hit me right then. I knew what I could blog about. Miracles! That's what this book is about. A miracle. I would interview people and share their miracle stories on a blog.

In the meantime, my son, Andrew, once a newspaper photo journalist, had just completed his second year of a new job as social media manager for Elon University. I ran the miracle blog idea by him, and he was very positive and kept using the word "we" as he talked about how "we" would link this up with Facebook, Twitter, Instagram, etc.

I told my daughter, Faith, about it. She had been doing interviews for StoryCorps, heard on National Public Radio, and is now a search engine optimization specialist. She was on board for interviewing folks in Colorado, where she now lives.

Karen had been very reluctant to read the book over the years. It was too emotional. I couldn't put it out there though, until she read it. Since we'd moved to HHICC, her faith had strengthened, and she finally mustered the power to read it and offer great editing notes in a very short period of time. What could be better than to have your whole family working together to spread God's Word? Amazing.

As I circled the book and the blog in prayer, my writing and editing also became stronger. It was finally going to be worthy as an offering to God. It was all coming together. In God's time. I just had to be a little patient. Like for thirteen years.

As I finished up the writing, I discovered the book, *Miracles: What They Are, Why They Happen, and How They Can Change*

Your Life by Eric Metaxas, another incredible inspiration and confirmation of the need to share God's amazing work through the book and the blog.

Even though we now have a way to build a following with the blog, I decided not to continue to pursue publishing with a traditional house even if a good-size fan base is established. This was a humbling experience. Most authors I know who have been published by a big-name publisher look down on self-publishers. I know I did. However, since all proceeds from the sale of the book are donated to charities, I figured the more money we kept, the more God would get for His work. I could use a little humility anyway. So that's how we went this route and began Belief Books (www.beliefbooks.com), which we used to publish this book and where you can link up to the Miracle Box blog.

What a blessing it has all been to write this, and for God to have given me a new job in helping to spread His Word. I am very thankful. Psalms 96:3 says, "Publish His glorious deeds among the nations. Tell everyone about the amazing things He does." And that's exactly what I hope to do here.

CHAPTER ONE

Babies Like This

Was it too soon to call a funeral home? A priest? Our families?

Ultimately, we just waited quietly. My wife, Karen, in the bed. Me, stiff and straight, in the only chair. The institutional face of the hospital clock showed it was 5:00 p.m. Karen's maternity nurse, Kim, had been gone an hour.

I stared out the window at the setting sun. A wintry twilight of washed-out blues and grays spread across the sky. I wanted it to be over and yet to never come.

Suddenly I heard Karen gasp and I knew it had started. Turning, I saw her staring straight at me, eyes wide. "It's happening!" she exclaimed. Blood seeped bright red onto the sheet below her waist. Karen pulled up her knees and gripped them tightly. I moved quickly to the bed and pushed the call button hard waiting expectantly for Kim's voice.

"The baby is low," Karen warned. Beads of sweat now dotted her forehead. "I can feel it. It's ready to come out," she panted.

I pushed the button again. And again.

The bloodstain was spreading farther down the sheet. My heart beat wildly. I worked to steady my voice. "I'm going to get somebody," I said.

Karen groaned as she rocked back in the bed.

I dashed into the hall and nearly rammed right into Kim running from the other direction. Puffing for breath, her face flaming red against her white uniform, she flew past me into the room. "Karen's having contractions!" I called after her. "She says the baby's coming."

Kim didn't answer. She was pressing buttons and flipping switches on the console behind Karen's head. "Karen, are you doing all right?" she asked.

"Yes," Karen managed between pants. "I'm okay."

"You're going to do fine, hon." She was speaking quickly, pulling cords and pushing more buttons. "Just hang in there with me." Kim took Karen's hand. I moved around to the other side of the bed and held her other hand.

Suddenly a small army of nurses rushed in through the doorway, rolling carts of equipment in front of them. Ultra-white bright lights were snapped on overhead. Curtains were yanked around us, apparatus of all sorts was plugged in, everyone was moving in different directions. In the midst of all the movement, Kim's voice was calm. "Do you feel like you're ready to push?"

Karen breathed, "Uh-huh."

"Go ahead and push," Kim urged.

Karen strained and arched her back. She gave a high gasp. Instantly, Kim called out, "It's a girl!"

From across the room a nurse called back, "5:22."

Cradled in Kim's large, soft hands was something impossibly small. The only thing I had ever seen like this before was from biology class: a fetal pig, tiny and folded up in a jar of formaldehyde. I heard a little cry. The smallest of sounds. I wasn't sure if it was my imagination. But Kim immediately called out, "Baby cried!"

My heart leaped. Karen looked to me with a stunned smile. I knew we were thinking the exact same thing—*the baby was alive!*

Kim passed the minuscule form over to the other nurses. They surrounded the baby and it disappeared from our sight. As I tried to catch another glimpse, I noticed a woman in a pale yellow surgical gown off to the side, busily writing on a clipboard. She had short, light brown, almost crew-cut hair, and large glasses. The way she kept writing and studying the equipment, I guessed she was a technician.

The baby remained hidden in a corner among the machines and nurses. The woman in the pale yellow gown placed the clipboard on a table and walked over to the bed. Her skin was very smooth. She was young, with a look of intelligence and confidence. She leaned toward Karen and spoke in a low voice. "I'm Dr. Hecht, the neonatologist." There was a small turning-up of the corners of her mouth, not quite a smile. She bent down closer to Karen. "How are you doing?" she asked.

Karen replied breathlessly, "I'm fine. How is the baby?"

Dr. Hecht straightened and spoke slowly in distinct, measured sentences. "Your baby is very sick. She's extremely small and unable to breathe on her own. We're keeping her breathing and heart going by machine."

I thought, sick? Like with a disease? What a strange thing to say. The part about the machines keeping her alive I understood all too well.

Dr. Hecht paused and when she spoke again her tone had changed. Almost instructively, as if talking to a child, she said gently to Karen, "We are going to give her back to you to hold so that you can keep her warm as she passes on. That's really the best we can do."

Karen listened to what surely must have struck her as a swirling of words, then turned to me, a look of shock and disbelief on her face. I was enraged. *Keep her warm until she passes on!* Our daughter was alive! This was more than any of us had hoped for. We knew about the excellent neonatal intensive care unit. Why weren't we rushing her over there?

The hot shock and revulsion I felt at Dr. Hecht's words passed. A feeling of cold calm and control snapped into place. I looked directly across the bed at her and asked, "Aren't you going to take her down to the unit?"

For the first time, she looked my way. She answered in the same even tone, "No. She is very weak and very small. She weighs less than a pound. We do not usually admit babies this small into the unit." She paused and then continued in a lower voice. "Babies like this don't make it."

CHAPTER 2

Vacation Days

When you're a teacher like Karen and me, you learn early on in your career not to discuss vacation days with anyone outside the profession. It will not win you any friends.

Teachers are the envy of the rest of the working world on this one perk. In New Jersey, we even had two days off in early November to attend a statewide teachers convention. These days always fell on a Thursday and Friday, resulting in a nice long weekend.

The Thursday of that November convention weekend back in 1992, Karen and I were enjoying the simple but much-appreciated luxury of sleeping late. Our son, Andrew, was two years old, and "sleeping late" meant 7:30 a.m., but it was still way better than his usual 6:00 a.m. wake-up. At eleven o'clock, we were all still in our pajamas.

Andrew and I lay side by side, belly down on the carpet in the family room. Bright morning sunshine streamed through the bay window, illuminating the colorful foam brick castle we were building. Karen sat reading the paper in the big comfy chair near the window. It was as relaxing a morning as you were ever going to have with a two-year-old.

"What are you planning on doing while we're away this weekend? Besides sitting around watching TV and eating bonbons," she teased.

That was not quite me. I am a compulsive list maker and doer. I like nothing better than crossing stuff off of my to-do list. An empty, unscheduled weekend was an amazing opportunity. "Ha, ha. You know the hedge along the back fence? The one that looks like something out of a Grimm's fairy tale?"

"Yes," she chuckled. "You're cutting it down?"

"That's what I have in mind," I said. "When do you think you'll head out for DC?"

"We should leave here about eight tomorrow morning. I'll pick Debbie up and meet Susan in Maryland."

The three sisters—Karen, Susan, and Debbie—enjoyed getting together whenever they could, especially for trips. Andrew was coming along this time too. That would leave me at home on my own. I'd decided I was going to pass on the convention this year. After teaching for six years overseas in Scotland and Saudi Arabia, we had only been back in the US and in this house about a year. It had been an estate sale that sat empty for two years and there was still a ton to do.

"Mom. Look!" Andrew called. He balanced one more block on top of an already precarious tower. "This one's going to be gigantic." He had quite a vocabulary for a two-year-old.

Karen slipped out of the chair and got down next to him on the carpet. She stroked his soft brown hair and smiled. "Wow. That's great, pal." Only a small bulge in her pink robe revealed that she was now just over five months pregnant, about twenty-two weeks, our next baby due in March. "Are you going anywhere today?" I asked.

"Just food shopping. I want to get some snacks for the trip and stuff for here." She stood and stretched, then walked out of the room.

"This castle has got a moat," Andrew said. He moved some little plastic knights around to the front.

"A goat?" I teased.

"No, a moat!" he said sternly.

"A coat?" Yes. I am that annoying kind of father.

Dad! A moat!"

Oh, a moat. Good idea, buddy."

We continued to build. I couldn't help but look out the window. The trees in the front yard were ablaze with beautiful orange and red leaves. There were also plenty on the ground too. Maybe I should be raking before I started on the hedge. I glanced up casually and saw that Karen had come back in and was standing behind us, watching. I turned my body, and only then did I see her face.

Her mouth was set in a tight straight line. I knew that look. Something wasn't right. She turned and walked into the kitchen.

I got up quickly and followed. I found her leaning against the counter, arms folded across her chest. I asked in a low voice, "Is everything okay?"

At first, she didn't say anything. Then she gave a slight shrug and said, "There was just some blood."

I froze. Those dreaded words. Again.

Karen had been through three miscarriages. Two when we were in Saudi, before Andrew was born, and then, when we thought we had put the problem behind us, a third. Each of those times she had begun to tell me with that same sentence: "There was just some blood." But this couldn't be a miscarriage. Things were way too far along.

I took a deep breath, struggling to sound calm. "Maybe you should call the doctor," I suggested. "Just to check it out."

She gazed out the kitchen window into the backyard and remarked, "Well, it wasn't a lot of blood. Just some streaking."

In as casual a voice as I could muster, I persisted. "You might want to see what he says though."

Karen paused. She was not meeting my eyes. "Well, we'll see. I'm going to get changed." Then she walked up the stairs.

I returned to the family room and lay back down next to Andrew. I was uneasy. I didn't want to let the word enter my mind again, but it stuck. *Miscarriage.*

Ten minutes later Karen reappeared downstairs, fully dressed. She headed back into the kitchen while I continued trying to play with Andrew. I could hear the breakfast dishes clanking as she washed them in the sink. After a few minutes, though, she was on the phone, talking with her younger sister, Debbie. This went on for about thirty minutes, followed immediately by another call I couldn't hear.

Andrew hopped up. "I'm going to the bathroom!" he announced. He ran across the rug and hurried around the corner, nearly bumping into Karen. She came over and sat down. "I talked to Dr. Baumann," she said.

I was relieved to hear it. Dr. Stephen Baumann was Karen's ob-gyn. "What did he say?"

"That it's probably nothing, but to come in later today just to check things out."

"Sounds like a good idea." A quick office visit would give us both some peace of mind. Meanwhile, I headed outside to pull the tools from the garage and start the hedge work while Karen and Andrew went out shopping.

At around four, we put Andrew into his car seat and drove the five minutes to the obstetrician's office. Normally, we wouldn't have brought him, but there was no one around at that moment to watch him and I definitely wanted to be there with Karen.

We were happily surprised to find the waiting room almost empty. A nurse greeted us with a friendly wave and a smile. "Last appointment of the day," she said breezily. She ushered us into a neat, modern examining room. Andrew found the doctor's stool, clambered up, and discovered that it could spin. It was naptime and he was getting his last bursts of energy out.

The nurse began to write on a clipboard. "So, what brings you here today?"

Karen replied, "It's just I've had some discharge recently. I called Dr. Baumann and he told me to come in."

"That's not uncommon. Lie right down here." She patted the examining table. "You look very good, Karen." Mentioning the discharge did not seem to alarm her at all. Already I was feeling better about this. "So, according to our chart, you're in about your twenty-second week, right?" She hooked Karen up to the fetal monitor and sat down next to her on a stool.

Yes," Karen answered.

She nodded and smiled. "And you've been feeling well?"

Yes. Fine."

"Excellent." And then she stopped talking and sat motionless for a moment, staring at the monitor. Andrew hopped off the stool and found his way to my lap, sucking his thumb and nodding sleepily.

In a hesitant voice the nurse asked, "Karen, have you felt any contractions?"

Karen paled. "N-n-no, I don't think so."

The nurse's smile had vanished. "It looks like you might be having some." She got up and stepped briskly to the door. "I'll get Dr. Baumann."

CHAPTER 3

Buying Time

K aren and I barely had a chance to look at each other before the examining room door swung open and Dr. Baumann appeared. He was tall and slim, in his late thirties, with dark brown hair and a trim mustache.

He gave me a nod, then turned to Karen. "I understand you may be having some contractions, Karen. Let's take a look."

He walked over to a small sink, carefully washed his hands, and slipped on gloves. I was glad to see he wasn't rushing. Maybe you could have some contractions early on in a pregnancy and that was okay.

He moved his arm under the sheets that fell across Karen's lap. He focused his eyes on a point on the wall and spoke calmly. "You've begun to dilate. You're about two to three centimeters now. The baby has started to descend."

Descend?!

Dr. Baumann peeled off his gloves, tossed them in a trash can, and washed his hands again. His tone remained calm, but his speech was slower, more deliberate. "Karen, why don't you get dressed and then we can all meet in my office and talk. I'll be right there."

He left. Karen pulled on her jeans and sweater. Neither of us spoke. The same nurse came back in and led us silently down the hall to a comfortable office. A large picture window overlooked the street. We sat down in two deep leather chairs across from a handsome wood desk as Andrew slept peacefully in my lap.

Dr. Baumann stepped in, a long manila folder under his arm. He closed the door and sat carefully behind his desk with hands folded in front. "I have to be honest with you," he said huskily. "Things don't look very good."

I'd never, ever heard a doctor say those words before.

He paused, nodding slightly toward Karen. "You're already dilated two centimeters. You're only about twenty-two weeks pregnant. If we can get you to twenty-four or twenty-five weeks, we'll be in a lot better shape, so I'm going to admit you to the hospital immediately and we will try to slow things down."

He looked to Karen, then to me. When we didn't respond, he stepped in to fill the stunned silence. "Right now, though, I would have to say that the baby will probably be born within a week."

My body felt like it was filling with cold water. This wasn't even a miscarriage. It was a birth he was talking about.

Dr. Baumann continued in a somber, steady tone. "This is very, very early, and unfortunately…there's a good chance the baby won't make it through labor and delivery."

Those sad words hung in the air, like a heavy, dark cloud. He again deliberately looked to Karen and then to me, like he was waiting for us to respond in some way—to ask a question, to say something, to cry, to show we understood—but neither of us moved.

He stood up. We did the same. "Don't go home. I want you to go directly from here to the hospital now. I've called admissions and they're ready for you. I'll meet you there."

He paused again, looking us over. All I could manage was, "Okay."

Karen was pale and expressionless.

"I'm really sorry," he said.

Andrew slept on, curled in a ball in my arms. In a few minutes, he would be continuing his nap at my parents' house. Karen, instead of going to Washington, was headed for Mercer Medical Center in Trenton.

During the short drive to the hospital, we held hands a few times at stoplights, but didn't say much. I was in shock. This was the kind of thing that happened to other people. Not us. I parked and we walked in the emergency room entrance together. As the automatic doors slid open, I looked around, almost surprised by my surroundings. I couldn't remember actually driving there.

The receptionist asked, "Can I help you?"

Karen stepped forward. "I'm Karen Krech, my doctor..."

"Yes." She turned to an orderly. "John, please take Mrs. Krech up to the third floor."

Karen was ushered into a wheelchair and over to a waiting elevator. I quickly reached out and we touched hands. "Kar, I'll be right up."

"Okay. I'm fine," she said and forced a smile.

Then she was whisked away. The receptionist pointed to her right. "Mr. Krech, you can go to admissions right down this hall."

I thanked her and followed the signs, passing through a door and into an open area that looked like someone's living room. Dark wood chairs and coffee tables sat serenely on a nice blue carpet. Nautical paintings hung on the walls. The admissions clerk was an older African American woman who beckoned me over to sit at her window. "How are you, dear? How can I help you today?" she asked warmly.

Her welcoming, casual manner allowed me to feel for a few minutes that I was just there to do a little paperwork. The questions about insurance and employment were so benign and easy, while everything else was rapidly spinning out of control.

After ten minutes, she smiled her final smile, though, and said, "You can go through those doors and then take the elevator up to the third floor. Good luck, now."

Part of me wanted to get right up there to be with Karen, but at the same time, another small part of me liked being right where I was, comfortably removed from everything. I walked slowly to the double doors and pushed.

The carpet abruptly ended. In front of me a floor of white speckled linoleum, covered with color-code trails of blue and green dots, opened up. Televisions murmured in waiting areas, mingling with a steady din of PA announcements and pages for doctors.

Nurses and technicians in pale blues and yellows hustled by, carrying clipboards and pushing equipment. The strong smell of disinfectant filled the air. Attendants moving patients in wheelchairs and on gurneys maneuvered past me.

When I reached the third floor, I found Karen already situated, alone in a room, wearing a gown and lying propped up with pillows in a bed. We joined hands. "Are you doing all right?" I asked.

"Yes," she said quietly. "At least now if something happens, I feel like I'm safe. I'm in the right place."

I sat down next to her on the bed and breathed a sigh. "Definitely." We had made it to the hospital, but now what? A minute later, Dr. Baumann walked in, his winter coat still on. It was reassuring to see him there so quickly.

He took the coat off, placed a black medical bag on a chair, and opened it. "Okay. Our primary objective now is to delay this birth as long as we can. That way we give the baby as much time as possible to grow and mature. I'm going to give Karen an injection of Brethine. This is to relax the uterus and stop any further contractions."

He readied the needle and gently administered the injection. He put that syringe aside and took another. "This second injection is betamethasone, which will help mature the baby's lungs so that if a birth were to take place soon, the baby would have a better chance."

He finished and put his things back in his bag. He stood up with his hands folded in front of him. "Tomorrow morning, we'll do a cerclage. This is an operation where we stitch the cervix closed. We'll push the sac back up into the uterus and hope that it will all hold in place till the baby is at least a few weeks more mature. In the meantime, Karen, you'll be on complete bed rest here at the hospital."

Karen asked, "For how long?"

"As long as possible, until things stabilize. It could be weeks or even months if we can get that far. The longer we can manage to hold off this delivery, the better," he said. He paused and looked from Karen to me. "We are simply buying time."

CHAPTER 4

Wait and Rest

K aren and I mutely nodded our understanding. Dr. Baumann slipped his coat back on, picked up his bag, and took a step toward the door, pausing there. He seemed reluctant to leave, as if there were more he wanted to say or do. "Good luck, guys," he said finally. "I'll see you tomorrow."

We thanked him and he was gone. It had taken all of ten minutes. Karen broke the silence in a small voice. "It sounds like he knows what he's doing," she said. "This could all still work out."

After what we we'd heard in Dr. Baumann's office, I braced myself for the worst, but I was glad Karen was hopeful. I didn't want to quash that. "Yeah. I think so," I replied.

We fell quiet again. I was trying to think of what I could do. What I should do. "We should probably call our parents," I offered.

"Yes. Why don't you go ahead first," she replied.

We took turns using the phone, letting our families know what was going on. It seemed unreal that I was here in a hospital telling my mother and father that we were about to have a baby, four months before the due date, while just a few hours ago I had been lying on the floor in our family room building castles with Andrew. It was all happening too fast.

When we were done, I sat down on the bed and held Karen's

hand. "Would you like me to stay here tonight?" I asked.

She shook her head. "No. I'd rather you go and take care of Andrew. I don't want him scared. I'm fine. Really."

"All right. I'll be back first thing in the morning."

We hugged and kissed good night. Then I drove to my parents' to pick Andrew up. I was hoping when I got home there wouldn't be a message waiting from Karen. I was hoping that everything would just stop. Just please stop.

•••

I woke up early the next morning after a restless sleep, packed up some things Karen had asked for, and brought Andrew back to my parents. I was at the hospital by seven.

Soon after I got back to her room, another of the ob-gyn group partners, Dr. Mark Druker, walked in. Dr. Druker had delivered Andrew. Over six feet tall and thin, he was the youngest of Karen's doctors. He reviewed Karen's situation with us, basically repeating all the things Dr. Baumann had told us. As he spoke, he paced back and forth. When he stopped moving, he finished by saying, "Even if the cerclage works and we get a few more weeks, there could still be many problems."

He didn't elaborate, which was just as well because I didn't want to think about it. I was already imagining very bad scenarios on my own. He rubbed his hands tightly together and looked at the floor a lot. "We'll do the best we can, of course," he said.

I had never seen a doctor so visibly nervous before. It scared me. When the nurses came and took Karen out on the gurney, I sat back down in the chair and prayed silently over and over. *Please help us. Please stop the birth.* My mind wandered again. What should I do? What could I do? The answer was the same as before. Basically—nothing.

After the cerclage was completed and Karen had returned to the room, Dr. Druker joined us again. He appeared more settled. "That went very well," he said. "Everything we can do at this point has been done. Now Karen just needs to rest."

And wait, I thought.

The maternity ward took up most of the third floor at Mercer, which made it an upbeat kind of place for a hospital. Instead of being surrounded by people who were sick or injured or elderly, the patients in Karen's wing were almost all healthy younger women. Happy chatter, laughter, and families filled the hallways.

We had breakfast and then lunch in the room. Karen was sitting up in bed reading. She looked completely normal.

"Seems like you're doing all right," I commented.

"I feel fine. Really."

I let a small glimmer of hope rise up. "That's good to hear."

She gripped my hand and smiled. "I know. I'm so thankful."

Later in the afternoon, Karen's sister Debbie, a recent college graduate, came up to visit. The two of them chatted about books and shared family gossip. It had been twenty-four hours now and nothing new had happened. That night when I went home and rejoined Andrew, I began to feel the first small tinges of relief.

I was back at the hospital early Saturday morning, November 7. Dr. Baumann and Dr. Druker arrived just after breakfast. I sat and watched as Dr. Baumann did an exam. At the conclusion, he let a smile escape. "All of your signs are unchanged. There's no further dilation. No more contractions," he said.

Both doctors were visibly pleased. "You have a lot of weeks of bed rest ahead of you, but this is good," Dr. Baumann remarked. As the doctors left, one of the young nurses on the floor remained. "You are doing really well and your doctors are the best," she said. Everyone was smiling. It was all under control. Thank goodness.

I spent the day hanging out with Karen. She was reading, talking on the phone, and napping comfortably. As I drove home, I reflected on how quickly Dr. Baumann had acted. How there had been things he could do to stop the birth and that they had worked. I slept much more peacefully.

On Sunday morning, Andrew and I went to church at nine. Karen and I were Catholic and had been regular churchgoers since childhood. Andrew was handling his mom's absence very well and bounced around as happy as ever, especially because of all the extra time he was getting over at his grandparents' house.

We had lunch and then headed over to the hospital. I kept him in his spiffy church outfit: dark blue dress pants, white shirt, and shiny brown shoes. Karen would enjoy seeing Andrew all decked out. As we drove, Andrew asked, "Is Mom sick?"

"No, buddy. She's just resting where the doctors can help her if she needs it."

"Oh." A nervous look crossed his face. "Will I have to see the doctors?"

I had to laugh. "No, pal. You're fine." Andrew smiled back.

We stopped in the hospital gift shop and bought a small

bouquet of bright yellow and blue flowers. I handed them to Andrew and we got on the elevator. His eyes grew wide and as we went up.

When we stepped out and turned the corner onto Karen's hall, I spotted the young nurse who yesterday had commented on how well Karen was doing. I gave her a friendly wave. She did not wave back. Instead she stood for a second in the middle of the hall staring at us, then walked hastily across to the nurses' station.

That was not normal. I quickened my steps to the room.

Karen was sitting up in bed, looking straight ahead. As we entered, she turned toward us. Her eyes were brimming with tears. Andrew, not noticing, skipped across the floor, thrusting the flowers in front of him. "Hi, Mom!"

"Ohhhh. Hi, buddy," she said through a chuckle and a sob. "Thank you for the beautiful flowers," she choked.

He hugged her and began an earnest search of the room for something to play with.

Karen looked up at me. "My water broke."

CHAPTER 5

Delivery Room

Are you all right?" I asked. She nodded and sniffed. I sank down onto the bed and took her hand. "When did this happen?"

Karen brushed the tears away with the back of her other hand. "Last night," she said. Her words were hesitant and soft. "I woke up with a pain in my lower left side. I knew right away it was a contraction." She paused, swallowing hard. "I started to panic and called the nurse. She was there right away...and listened with a stethoscope. She said it sounded like gas to her. I wanted to believe her, but..."

She looked small and vulnerable in the big, loose hospital gown. "Then this morning at about ten..." She paused and wiped away more tears. "I was waking up and repositioning when I felt a small gush of fluid down my legs. I didn't call anyone to tell them." She shook her head. "I didn't want to believe it was happening."

She continued, choking out the words. "When the nurse came to take my morning temperature, I finally told her. She did a litmus test and said it looked like it might be amniotic fluid, but...that the test wasn't always accurate. I tried to call you, but you must have already left the house."

"What are you guys talking about?" Andrew interrupted.

Karen laughed a little through her tears. "Nothing, buddy."

I picked up the phone by the bed and called my parents. I spoke to my father, filling him in and asking him to come over and get Andrew as soon as he could. He arrived at Karen's door within twenty minutes. We shook hands. My dad was not a hugger. Andrew spotted him and came running. "Pop!" he shouted and leaped into his arms.

"Thanks for coming, Dad," I said. "I'll keep you posted on what's happening."

"Okay," he said.

"Andrew, you can sleep at Grandma and Grandpa's tonight," I told him.

"Yes!" he cheered. He then leaped down and danced joyfully in a little circle. Karen and I hugged Andrew tightly before he headed to the door. As my father and Andrew left, she said out loud exactly what I was thinking privately: "Thank God we have him. At least we have Andrew."

But what happens now? I thought. What about *this* baby?

A few minutes later, Dr. Baumann appeared. "Let's check on things here. It sounds like maybe you had some fluid discharge."

He did a quick exam. "Yes, your water broke," he said flatly. It was the same somber tone we had heard in his office on Thursday. "I'm going to take the stitch out now since it can't help any longer. It will only be in the way. Labor should ensue soon after, probably within the next few hours."

As he did this, he continued talking. "Since the sac had been exposed to the air, what probably happened was that it started to deteriorate. Nothing really could stop it from there."

All the anticipation of Karen being in the hospital for weeks while the baby grew and strengthened, all the dreams of visits and presents and a safe delivery weeks or months down the road vanished. The baby would be born today.

Dr. Baumann walked toward the door. "I'm going to arrange for the delivery room. Hang in there." And he was gone.

I sat back down on the bed. We held hands again. I said, "It'll be okay."

"I know." Karen nodded and sniffed. She repeated, "We still have Andrew."

We were about to lose a child and our only comfort was that we still had Andrew and each other.

We hugged and held for a long time. Finally, Karen lay down and I got up and sat in a chair. None of the miscarriages had been easy, but this time it would be far worse. Karen would give birth and then the baby would die.

We sat silently adrift in our own thoughts. Should I call a funeral director? Or was it too soon to do that? What would we tell Andrew? Should we even tell him anything?

Karen sat up suddenly. "Bob. I'm feeling more contractions."

I moved up and out of my chair. "I'll get someone," I blurted. I walked quickly into the hall. The one nurse there looked up from her desk. I tried to keep my voice steady, but it came trembling out. "My wife is having more contractions."

She stood up. Her expression didn't change. "Let's move to a delivery room."

I noticed the big wall clock above her desk. It was 1:00 p.m. She grabbed a wheelchair and I followed behind her back to the room. She handed me a large plastic bag. "You can put her things in here."

I gathered Karen's few belongings, then the three of us headed out into the hall. We went through two large, heavy wooden doors and into an area in the midst of being renovated. Plastic tarps were draped from ceiling to floor in places. Ladders, drop cloths, and construction materials were everywhere.

We passed a large nurses' station. A few nurses glanced up quickly, then returned just as quickly to studious scrutiny of whatever was in front of them. Maybe they already knew who we were and that we were on our way to the place where a baby would die.

We walked by one empty room after the other, doors wide open, lights off, but we didn't stop till we reached the last room at the end of the long, quiet hall. The lights were on but dimmed and it was icy cold. "You can lie down there, Karen," the nurse said, gesturing to the empty bed.

Karen climbed out of the wheelchair and into the bed. She immediately pulled up the sheets. The nurse retreated, but paused at the door. She remained calm and neutral, almost passive. "Someone will be along soon," she said. "Good luck."

"Thanks," I mumbled.

It was a simple room. The large hospital bed, a chair, one thin window. A few minutes later, Dr. Baumann came in. He put a hand on Karen's shoulder. "It'll probably be a few more hours," he said. "I'll be available. Have them page me when you need me." He shook hands with both of us. "Hang in there," he said again. And then he was gone.

We were only alone for another minute before a large nurse strode briskly into the room. "Hello," she called out in a cheery voice. She looked around and frowned. "Oh my. It's a little dim in here." She turned the lights up. "That's better," she said.

She was one of those people who, though big, move quickly and delicately. She spoke sort of breathlessly as she quickstepped over to the bed. "I'm Kim and I'm going to help you out here today."

Kim was built wide with short blonde hair, a reddish face, and large glasses perched on a small nose. She looked to be in her mid-thirties, about our age. She pulled up a chair next to the bed and smiled at Karen. In an upbeat voice, she said, "So, this is kind of early, but you look like you're doing well."

"Yeah." Karen forced a smile.

We chitchatted briefly about where we were from, our families, and our jobs. It was a strange, quick getting-to-know-you, but Kim was bringing some welcome warmth into that cold, desolate room. She patted Karen's hand. "Dr. Baumann is excellent. I'm sure you'll do fine."

Karen would do fine? What did that mean? And what about the baby? From Kim's demeanor and the way she was talking, I got the impression she might not have been informed completely about our situation. "The baby is very premature," I said abruptly.

She nodded. "Right. I know."

"What if the baby doesn't make it?" I asked. It was a blunt, raw question, but there was no time left. I needed to know.

Kim paused. Almost reluctantly, she said, "Well, I have some information here." She reached in a drawer and pulled out a light blue pamphlet. She handed it to me. Stapled on top was a small white note with a list of the hospital's chaplains and their phone numbers. The Catholic chaplain was listed first. It was a Father O'Brien from Blessed Sacrament Church in Trenton. But I already had a parish priest. I flipped the note up to reveal the title of the pamphlet: *Dealing with a Child's Death*.

While Kim talked to Karen, I quickly skimmed the booklet. It talked about loss. About counseling. About ways to remember your child. I quickly put it down. I wanted to know, but I didn't want to know.

After giving us some more encouragement, Kim walked to the door and motioned to the hall. "I'll be right around here if you need me. Just ring the call bell." And she was gone too.

Karen and I sat quietly for a minute. We were about to lose a child and all we could do was sit there and wait for it to happen. Then Karen abruptly sat up. "The contractions are starting again," she said.

I moved to the bed. "Should I call someone?"

"No. Not yet." She swallowed heavily and sat back. "It's going to be a while yet."

I sat back down too. Then I stood up and leaned against the windowsill. I walked over to Karen. I couldn't find the right place or way to be. A baby was going to be here, in this room, soon. Our baby. I had to broach a subject with Karen that I had been holding back on. Finally, I just asked her, "Karen, do you think we should talk about a name for the baby?"

She shook her head immediately, like she had been waiting for this. She wiped away more tears. "I can't. No," she sobbed.

I understood. If we gave the baby a name, it would be a person. A real part of our family. It would make the death hurt even more.

CHAPTER 6

Birth

But the baby was not dead. And now, this neonatologist who had been in the delivery room all of five minutes, this *Dr. Hecht*, had just had the audacity to tell us that she was not even going to try to keep our baby alive—because it was too small.

I couldn't believe this was really going to happen. "You're basing this on weight?!" I exclaimed.

Dr. Hecht did not respond. Instead a steely silence hung in the air between us. Two nurses stood motionless directly behind her. The tall, dark-haired one was looking at me, her eyes wet. She moved her head in an almost imperceptible nod. Maybe another second passed. No one said a thing.

I was not thinking; I just blurted out, "You're kidding!"

Karen implored her, "The baby is alive. Aren't you going to do something?"

Dr. Hecht held herself tight and straight. She seemed to be measuring us or weighing something. Finally, in a neutral voice she said, "All right." And then added pointedly, "I will take her down at your direction."

I wasn't thinking about any of the implications of this other than that our baby was alive and we should try to keep her alive. "Fine," I said.

Dr. Hecht turned and began to direct the nurses. They placed the baby in what looked like an incubator on wheels, and as suddenly as they had arrived, the whole group and all the equipment were gone. Only Kim remained behind with us.

It was as if a tornado had blown into the room, whirled everything around, and blew out again, leaving a silent vacuum in its wake. I felt incredible relief. The confrontation was over. The baby was alive and she would get help now. Kim and I turned our attention to Karen.

Karen looked at me and smiled. "She's alive," she said. I hugged her. We both began to cry. The baby was alive!

Kim tried repeatedly to reach Dr. Baumann, but couldn't. Instead, a few minutes later, the obstetrician on duty tiptoed hesitantly into the room. She appeared shy and didn't say much, didn't even introduce herself, just smiled and said in a heavy Filipino accent, "I am going to remove the placenta now."

After a few minutes of trying to do just that, it was clear it was not going well. Karen groaned in pain as more blood stained the sheets. I was about to ask her to stop when, mercifully, Dr. Baumann showed up, tapped the other doctor on the shoulder, and said, "Thank you. I'll take it from here."

The woman smiled, bowed slightly, and exited. Dr. Baumann did a quick exam and said, "Karen's lost some blood here. She's okay, but I'm going to take her to the OR to finish this up under general anesthesia."

Two nurses appeared at the door. Karen and I gripped hands until they wheeled her out right in the bed. Dr. Baumann remained.

"They're going to get her prepped," he said. "Don't worry. Karen will be fine."

That was a relief. Now I could tell him about the baby. I was excited and had to work to keep my voice on an even keel. "The baby was born alive. They have her down in the NICU now."

Dr. Baumann's response to my excitement was to look down at the floor and then up at me. He took a breath. "Bob," he said quietly. "We're going to do our best here, but you have to understand. Even though the baby was born alive, her chances of surviving are still not very good at all."

He might as well have put his hands on my shoulders, pushed me into a chair, and said, "Settle down. Don't kid yourself." All the air went out of me. "Right," I said. "I know."

"I'm going to go finish up with Karen now," he said. "I'll see you in a bit. You can wait back in Karen's room. We can talk more then."

"Thanks." I gave him a small wave as he moved off and then I was alone.

I picked up Karen's solitary plastic bag and turned my back on the cold room. Walking down the hallway, I stopped at a window and stared out onto an empty, dark city street. Dr. Baumann's message was clear. Though the baby had been born alive, she was not going to make it. And we had forced them to try anyway.

I made my way back through the long hall of tarps and construction and past the nurses' station. I was glad to be out of that cold, sad place, but Karen's room had a different feel now. The happy mental picture I had painted of returning there on sunny days for pleasant visits with friends, relatives, magazines, books, and gifts had evaporated.

I put the bag down and called Karen's mother and my parents to update them. These were succinct and tearful conversations. Basically, I said, "The baby was born at about five thirty. She is alive...but it doesn't look good." That's about all I could think to say. "I'll keep you posted as things happen."

My mother said, "I am praying for her."

My father asked, "Do you want us to come over there?"

"No," I replied instantly. "No. Not yet. I'll let you know."

I didn't want anyone else near this. I didn't want them to be hurt any more than need be. I did want our parish priest here though. Or at least I wanted to talk to him. I needed advice on issues like last rites and the burial. I called but got a recording. I left a message asking him to call the hospital. I would find out later that he was away that weekend and would never receive the message.

I pulled out the pamphlet with the list of hospital chaplains Kim had given me. I called the Catholic chaplain, Father O'Brien, and got his phone machine too. I left another message. We were still on our own.

I sat on the edge of the bed waiting for Karen's return. This was going to be on me. I was the one who'd demanded intervention from Dr. Hecht, but I knew Karen wanted the same thing. Now I realized we had just delayed the inevitable.

A nurse looked in. "Your wife is in the recovery room. You can follow me down."

We walked together to a small room where Karen and three other women lay on big wheeled beds. High in one corner, a television was showing *The Frank Sinatra Story*. Normally I would have been at least mildly interested, with Sinatra being from Hoboken, New Jersey, and my own family roots right next door in Jersey City. Instead, I felt an irrational annoyance. Who cared about a second-rate made-for-TV movie?

I held Karen's hand. "Hey," I said in a low voice. "How are you doing?"

She spoke drowsily. "I'm all right. Do you know anything about the baby?"

"No. Nothing yet."

"Oh," she said and then immediately drifted back to sleep. I watched her for a few minutes then released her hand.

The nurse said, "She'll be like that for a while yet."

"I understand," I replied. There was nothing else I could do there, and it was very crowded, so I backed up and said, "I'm going to walk a bit."

I went into the hall and there was Dr. Baumann. He said, "Karen did fine. She lost some blood. She's a little weak, but she's in good shape."

He gestured for me to follow him to a quiet area away from the recovery room. He stopped there and looked at me expectantly. I'm sure he sensed that a new and even greater concern was on my mind. I began, "Look. I know the baby is being kept alive by machines and you've been saying things don't look very good. I was wondering though..." It was hard to frame the question, but I stumbled on. "Will we know? How will we know…?" I tried to keep my voice normal, but I was choking up.

"It will be clear," he reassured me. "A point comes when you know they're suffering needlessly. It becomes obvious. We'll all know. You'll know."

I wanted to believe him. I trusted these doctors, or at least I wanted to trust them, but I was also painfully aware that I had already gone totally against a specialist's counsel only half an hour ago on the same life-or-death decision.

Dr. Baumann interrupted my thoughts. "You can go see the baby now," he said.

I was taken totally off guard. If anything, I thought they would want to keep me away. He pointed to a solid wooden door. "In there. They're expecting you. I'll be around if you need me," he said.

I was surprised he wasn't coming with me, but I went on ahead and walked cautiously through the door into a small anteroom. Against one wall were a long stainless-steel sink and an open closet with a row of yellow gowns. Straight ahead was another door with a small window and black lettering—NICU. Through the window I could see nurses, incubators, and equipment.

I didn't know if I was allowed to just walk in, so I peered through the window until a nurse noticed me. She waved. Maybe she had been there at the birth. It had all been so quick and there had been so many nurses, I couldn't be sure.

The nurse joined me in the anteroom. She was small and young, with a long brown ponytail. "Hi, Mr. Krech. I'll just show you how to scrub up and then we can go and see your baby."

She knew my name. She must have been there. We scrubbed side by side in the huge sink, soaping up and working the hot water with a foot pedal. It was nice to be with another person.

She took one of the gowns off a hook and handed it to me. "Here we go. Put this on and just follow me."

She pushed the bar that opened the door and we walked into a long room lined with incubators. A low-level din of beeping and ringing noises filled the air. I noticed a brown-and-blue bunny-rabbit border running around the ceiling edges, rocking chairs, and other surprising bits of coziness.

"She's right over there," the nurse said. Directly in front of us, I saw Dr. Hecht and a handful of nurses standing in a tight ring. They surrounded what appeared to be a tray suspended on a pole at about chest height. A large light above lit the tray with an intense whiteness, completely washing the color from the faces of the people gathered around it.

As I approached, they spontaneously opened the circle. Small nods and quiet hellos greeted me. I could see into the tray now. Amid a tangle of wires, tubes, and tape lay a tiny, emaciated body not much bigger than my hand.

The skin was purplish-red, every inch of it covered by a fine, light blonde hair, like a spiky translucent fur. The eyes were fused shut. Her limbs curled stiff and tight, moving in slow, spastic jerks. Her toes arched upward, thin and bony. The skin was stretched over her body like plastic wrap.

Our daughter.

CHAPTER 7

First Night

It was far easier to look at Dr. Hecht than at the baby. I had to ask her the obvious question. "How is she doing?"

Hidden deep in my heart I harbored a tiny, ridiculous hope that Dr. Hecht would say something like, "We're amazed. She's actually doing much better than we expected. She'll be fine."

"Your baby's seriously ill" was the real answer. "She's receiving a great deal of oxygen and doing no breathing on her own."

That was what I really expected and I knew what to do next. I asked, "Would it be okay to baptize her?"

My response was driven in part by growing up Catholic and having it drummed into my head that babies must get baptized, but even more so by my family's sad personal history with this sacrament.

Three years before I was born, I had an older sister, Judy, who had been stillborn. Judy was not baptized in the hospital, was not allowed to be baptized, or whatever the ridiculous, arbitrary Catholic church rule was back in the 1950s, but ultimately she'd had to be buried in a separate part of the cemetery away from the rest of my mother's family just because she hadn't been baptized. My mother never forgot or forgave and would still bitterly retell the story decades later.

Dr. Hecht's neutral expression did not change in the least. She replied, "Of course" and nodded to a nurse, who walked over to a nearby counter.

The nurse returned and handed me what looked like a baby food jar. A simple black-and-white label read STERILIZED WATER. The other nurses made room for me as Dr. Hecht stepped over to another incubator.

My hand shook a little as I broke the seal. I unscrewed the cap and dipped my thumb in. I tentatively made the sign of the cross on the baby's forehead, gently brushing against the fine blonde hairs. My voice quavered as I whispered, "I baptize you in the name of the Father, and of the Son, and of the Holy Spirit. Amen."

I was hoping to feel something at that point. A bit of closure maybe. Instead, I felt unsettled and I knew why. Baptisms include a name. How could she not have a name? But it was done. I passed the jar of water back to the nurse.

For the first time I noticed a hospital identification card taped to the end of the baby's tray. It was pastel pink and blue, sprinkled with drawings of rattles and cute teddy bears. In the blank for baby's name it read: GIRL KRECH. Her birth weight was listed as 450 grams. I would learn that day that there are 454 grams in a pound.

The other babies around us looked to me like giant infants in comparison, like miniature sumo wrestlers complete with cascading rolls of enviable baby fat.

The same tall, dark-haired nurse who had nodded to me during the delivery was in our circle. She introduced herself as Peg and we shook hands.

She then began explaining things in a slow, patient manner. "Your baby is in what we call a warmer, which is basically a tray under a heat lamp." She pulled a sheet of plastic wrap from one end of the tray and stretched it across to the other end. "This plastic helps keep her from losing water weight and drying out while the heat lamp keeps her body temperature up in a normal range. She can't control her own temperature yet."

I nodded as the words washed over me. I tried to focus on what she was saying while taking in this tiny writhing human that was our child.

"She's lying on a water bed covered with terry cloth and a blanket." She pressed it lightly with her finger so it rocked gently. "This is electrically warmed so it helps to replicate the feeling of being in the womb somewhat and keeps her comfortable."

It struck me as incredibly kind that in the midst of this life-and-death situation, they cared that the baby was comfortable.

Dr. Hecht was back. The overhead lights glinted off the steel rims of her glasses. She seemed neither glad nor unhappy to see me there. She looked at her clipboard and began writing. "What week was your wife in, Mr. Krech?"

"Today was the beginning of the twenty-third week."

Dr. Hecht abruptly looked up. "You're sure?"

"Yeah. Pretty sure. I can check with Karen."

She nodded and tucked the clipboard under her arm. "Here's our situation." She paused and looked at me gravely. "Your baby is unable to breathe on her own. At all. She is receiving air through a tube going into her mouth and threading down into her lungs. This keeps her alive, but unfortunately has very serious side effects. The air that is supplied by the respirator through the tube is about ninety-five to ninety-nine percent oxygen."

She gestured toward a machine with bright red digital read-outs. "This is what she requires right now to stay alive. Adults breathing room-air only require about twenty percent oxygen. This higher percentage of oxygen given over time will greatly damage the baby's eyes and eventually could lead to blindness."

I found myself picturing a blind child. For some reason sitting alone on a chair in a corner of our house. My blind child.

"However, we can't lower the percentage of oxygen unless the baby starts breathing more efficiently. Her lungs are very immature."

This jolted me out of my daydream. It didn't make sense. How could the baby have cried out if her lungs were so immature? "I heard her cry when she was born," I said.

Dr. Hecht contradicted me very directly. "You didn't hear her cry; you heard her gasp for air."

My neck stiffened. I was ready to argue about what I'd heard and what the nurse Kim had called out, but I thought better of it. It would not help anything to start debating with Dr. Hecht about what I'd heard or didn't hear.

She went on. "The respirator is not only supplying her with oxygen, but also inflating her lungs. We regulate the rate of breaths the machine gives her based on how much breathing she is doing on her own and her oxygen saturation level."

I stared at the respirator. It hummed and thumped in a seamless rhythm.

"Right now, the machine is doing all of her breathing for her. This keeps her alive, but will also eventually damage the lung tissue by continually stretching it to the point where the lungs lose all elasticity and she would then need the respirator permanently. Our job is to try to get her off as soon as possible."

She pointed to what looked like a red, glowing ball taped in the baby's hand. "This is her pulse oximeter. It relays to the monitor your daughter's pulse rate and the percentage of oxygen in her bloodstream. This percentage is her oxygen saturation level, or SAT number.

"We want to see the baby with blood oxygen saturation above ninety percent. Alarms are set on the machine so that if she goes below ninety or above ninety-eight, it will ring. If she falls below ninety, more oxygen will be administered via her respirator tube. If she goes above ninety-eight, we lower the oxygen mix. We have to maintain a balance."

I glanced down at the baby again. She was tensing her stick arms and legs, struggling jerkily. Like she was fighting something. Maybe fighting to breathe.

"Of course, we're also monitoring her heart rate and blood pressure." I looked up. Dr. Hecht was watching me. She continued when she saw she had my attention. "We're giving her fluids and all her medications through this tube inserted through the navel. We can't leave it there for too long though. It's an infection risk, but right now it's the only way we can give her what she needs. She's also getting a stimulant for her heart and lungs and antibiotics to help prevent infections."

I nodded understanding, but it was a tidal wave of information.

She asked me again about Karen's dates. She asked me if we were certain about them. I told her I was sure, but said again that I would check with Karen. Dr. Hecht consulted her clipboard once more. "Surprisingly, her blood gas levels are in the normal range."

Normal? I hadn't yet heard that word even once here. I asked cautiously, "Is that a plus?"

Her voice suddenly rose a bit. "It's a double plus. We will be monitoring the baby's blood gas levels continually until things stabilize, then we'll be checking every three hours. The blood gas tests show the amount of CO_2 in the blood and percentage of electrolytes like potassium and sodium. At this point, somehow the baby is managing to keep the electrolytes in her blood balanced and the CO_2 down to acceptable levels." She paused ever so slightly. "Babies at this gestation are not expected to be able to do this."

Then for the first time that night Dr. Hecht smiled a slight smile. "We've just got to keep praying," she said.

I wanted to grab her and hug her. No matter what she personally or professionally thought the baby's chances were, Dr. Hecht was praying for my child and working hard to keep her alive.

"Thank you," I said. "We really appreciate it."

She nodded and smiled again. "You can visit her whenever you want. You and your wife have twenty-four-hour access here."

"Thank you," I said again. "I'm going to go see Karen now." I felt it was time to get out of their way and let them do what they had to do uninterrupted. I turned from the warmer and strode to the door. I was excited. Everything I'd heard about the baby doing no breathing on her own, the chance of blindness, that was all pushed aside in my mind. The baby somehow had a "normal blood gas level." I clung to that.

When I returned to the recovery room, I found Karen awake and sitting in a wheelchair. I wheeled her back to her room where a nurse joined us from the hallway station and helped her into bed.

I told Karen about the baby and my conversation with Dr. Hecht. We sat on the bed together and I held her in my arms as we cried. I could feel how physically weak and tired she still was. "You better rest," I said.

She nodded. "I don't think I'm ready to see the baby yet."

"No," I replied, picturing the tiny, struggling form in the other room. That would not be a good idea.

A few minutes later, Karen's end of the conversation faded and she was asleep again. A nurse poked her head in. She looked at Karen and then over to me. "If you want to sleep in the other bed, I can bring you some scrubs."

"That would be really helpful. Thank you."

I also borrowed some paper from her and wrote out a set of basic substitute lesson plans for my class. Then I called my father from the hall phone to update him and see if he could come over in a couple of hours to pick up the plans and deliver them in the morning. He and my mother still had Andrew at their house. I missed Andrew badly. I wanted to just touch him and hold him.

As I lay on the bed, I decided I would try to see the baby every three hours through the night. Dr. Hecht said they would be taking blood samples and running tests at three-hour intervals, so it seemed to make sense as there might be some news at these times. More so, though, I had the irrational feeling that if I fell asleep or stayed away from the baby for too long, something would go wrong. It was like I was on watch.

But the tight knit of the wool blanket was warm and comforting. I curled snugly up in it. The NICU and our baby receded. As I drifted off, a thought went through my mind that when I woke up, everything would be back the way it was three days ago. Karen happily pregnant. Me lazily playing with Andrew. We wouldn't have a severely premature baby on the edge of dying. That bad dream would be over.

•••

When I woke again, it was pitch-black in the room. I felt the crisp, stiff sheets and itchy wool blanket tight around me. I was still in the hospital. My cozy, reassuring wish of time-turned-back slowly receded. The cold edge of reality nudged me awake. Our baby girl was still down the hall struggling to live.

I pushed the light button on my watch. The faint bluish glow revealed that it was just after 2:00 a.m. Early Monday morning, November 9.

My long vacation weekend was finally over.

CHAPTER 8

Visits

Climbing out of the bed, I fumbled my clothes on in the dark. I rode the elevator down to the lobby and waited by the front desk. This time of night everyone came in through the emergency room entrance. I had asked my father to meet me here though. Within a few minutes, the automatic doors from the parking lot slid open and he walked in, bundled in a long storm coat. He exchanged nods with the security guard there.

In his late sixties, my dad was gray-haired and lined, but sturdy. All of my friends growing up used to say, "Your father looks like a cop." A retired New Jersey state trooper, he had been through more than a few hospitals and to plenty of 2:00 a.m. emergencies in his career. He didn't look at all nervous or out of place here. If anything, it was familiar ground and it was good to see him.

We shook hands. "How is she?" he asked.

I tried to find the right words. "She's very weak, but they're doing everything they can."

He nodded.

I handed him the plans. "If you can drop these off at my school before eight o'clock, that would be great, Dad. Thanks."

"No problem," he said.

We stood there for another second. Then spontaneously I

asked, "You want to see her?"

I think he was taken off guard. After the slightest pause, he said, "Yeah. Okay."

I led the way back, showing him where to scrub up and the gowns we had to wear. When we stepped into the brightly lit reality of the NICU, I saw that the ring of nurses and Dr. Hecht were still packed tightly around the baby's warmer. My fear returned full force. What was I bringing my dad into?

Noticing us, the circle opened once again.

I introduced my father to Dr. Hecht and asked how the baby was doing.

In response, she consulted her clipboard. "Nothing new to report except her official condition is now listed, which is critical."

The tall, dark-haired nurse, Peg, was still there. She smiled at me and added softly, "She is jaundiced so we do have the bili lights set up here." She pointed at them above the tray. "Everything else is pretty much the same."

At least jaundice was something I'd heard of. Three days ago, jaundice would have been a big deal. Now it was a welcome familiarity. My father stood there, bending slightly down at the baby, taking it all in. I watched him and wondered if he would be visibly shocked or saddened. If he would tear up or turn away.

But when he raised his head, he was smiling. Maybe it was a nervous smile or one of awe, or maybe, like me, despite all the fear and strangeness, he was genuinely happy on some level. Happy for the simple reason that she was alive and so there was still hope.

I looked back down at the baby again too. So impossibly small and frighteningly thin. But then for the first time it also occurred to me that she was an incredibly detailed and perfect baby. Her nose, her hands, her fingernails—there were no deformities.

Even so, it was uncomfortable to watch her for too long. She kept writhing and contorting her body. She looked distressed.

After about ten minutes, we said our goodbyes and thanks. It felt strange to just stand there and stare for too long. Back out in the hall, my dad filled me in on what Andrew had been up to. Then we shook hands, holding on just a little longer than usual. My father had a funny expression on his face. "You okay?" I asked.

"Yeah," he said. Then he added, a touch of wonder in his voice, "It's pretty amazing, isn't it?"

"Yeah, it is." It was true. The smallest human being either of us had ever seen or probably ever would see. We both shook our heads at the strangeness of it all. "Well, take care, Dad. Thanks again for doing this."

"No problem," he said. He walked out into the night and I went up again to the third floor.

Back in Karen's room, I changed and lay down on my bed. I could not shut my brain off. I seesawed back and forth. She's going to make it. She had a normal blood gas. She's going to live! Don't be stupid. Accept it. She's going to die. Don't dare hope where there is none or you will be devastated with disappointment.

I could hear Karen tossing fitfully on the other side of the room. I tried to pray again, but my prayers were interrupted by unwanted scenes bubbling up in my mind: The inevitable knock at the door and a nurse asking us to come quickly. We needed to come quickly and see the baby. She was slipping fast. We needed to say goodbye. I felt it coming.

Finally, a pale morning light seeped through the blinds. It was 6:00 a.m. Karen was sleeping deeply. I felt tired and heavy, but I dressed and went back into the NICU. There was Dr. Hecht, still in the same pale yellow gown. She had worked through the night.

I walked up and asked the pointed, unavoidable question, "How is she doing?"

Dr. Hecht surprised me with another small smile. She shook her head as she spoke. "She's hanging in. She's a fighter."

A fighter! Hanging in!

She pointed to one of the monitors. "The amount of oxygen we're giving her is still dangerously high, but unfortunately there's not a lot we can do there." She gave a small sigh. "She has to pick up and take over more of the breathing, but right now, she's just not assisting at all."

Dr. Hecht tilted her head slightly. "Looking ahead, statistically her chances will increase significantly if she can survive the first twenty-four hours."

Though it felt like days had passed, it had only been thirteen hours.

"Then if we can get her to the seventy-two-hour mark, her odds will greatly increase. If she can get that far, she would be considered viable."

"What does that mean exactly—'viable'?" I asked.

Dr. Hecht ran a finger along an eyebrow. "That she has the capability to survive."

Meaning, right now she didn't.

Dr. Hecht asked me once again about Karen's dates, and I said that I had checked with Karen and that she was sure that she had just started her twenty-third week on the day the baby was born. Yesterday.

As I spoke, she wrote carefully on her ever-present clipboard. Dr. Hecht turned to Peg. "Would you please give Mr. Krech some of the literature on prematurity?"

Dr. Hecht and I shook hands and she moved on to another baby. Peg returned and handed me three pamphlets. I took the opportunity to ask her about Dr. Hecht's continued interest in Karen's dates.

"Oh yes," she said. "Treatment is very specific to the gestational maturity of the baby. What week was your wife in?"

"Twenty-second, starting the twenty-third yesterday," I said.

She shook her head. "Oh. I don't think that could be right," she said. "I've seen twenty-two-weekers. Their skin is like paper." She pointed at the baby's chest. "You couldn't put these sticky monitor tabs on and off without ripping it. Look at her skin. It's too good for a twenty-two-week-old. Also, she couldn't be breathing like this. At twenty-two weeks, a baby's lungs are just buds. They can't really function at all."

Now I understood Dr. Hecht's continued focus on the dates. Still, Karen was sure that the dates were correct. Certainly Dr. Baumann, who had followed the baby's progress during Karen's prenatal care, had the same dates.

It appeared, though, that the baby's lungs were more developed than they should be, and her skin was also more fully developed than expected. This, in addition to the normal blood gas readings that had surprised Dr. Hecht, made three significant positive developments. Like three little miracles.

I was excited. I made my way back to the room at seven just as Karen was waking up. I sat on the side of her bed and took her hand. "Morning, Kar. How are you doing?" I asked quietly.

Karen rubbed the sleep from her eyes. She brushed the hair from her face. "I'm feeling stronger than last night. How's the baby?"

I launched into an enthusiastic retelling of the three positives I was now clinging to. I didn't want to build Karen up only to see her knocked down. It had only been thirteen hours. The baby was being kept alive with machines. She wasn't breathing on her own. But to my mind, there were amazing things happening.

Karen listened, then said, "I think I feel strong enough to see her." As she said this, she got up and wrapped herself in the big pink terry-cloth bathrobe I'd brought from home. She moved slowly.

"Okay," I said. I was surprised that she was ready to do this. She sat down in the wheelchair, and I maneuvered it down the hall. We did the hand washing and gowned up. As we entered, Karen gazed around at the forest of medical machinery and the bustling nurses.

There was no one near the warmer. I pulled up and said, "She's right in there."

Karen pressed her lips together in that thin, taut, concerned line. She pushed herself up out of the wheelchair and teetered on her feet, peering over the edge of the tray. Her hair came forward around her face and she wobbled as she stood.

Then she got her first real look at the little writhing red form in the tray. She stood transfixed for a moment and then quickly sat right back down. Staring at the floor and blinking away tears, she said, "I'm ready to go back now."

As I wheeled Karen out of the NICU, I felt terrible. I had painted her a picture of miracle upon miracle and then brought her in there for her first stark closeup view of this poor, tiny, struggling stick of an infant. We were in the room only a few minutes when the phone rang. I answered it wondering who could be calling us here.

"Hello, Mr. Krech. This is Father O'Brien from Blessed Sacrament."

CHAPTER 9

A Name

Father O'Brien? Then I remembered that this was the name of the local priest I had called the night before.

"I got your message, Mr. Krech. Would you like me to come over there?"

I hesitated. I didn't know him at all. Still, we hadn't heard from our parish priest and with my own feelings bouncing wildly between hope and resignation, depression and elation, I felt I needed all the spiritual guidance I could get. I asked him to hold on. "Karen. It's the priest from down the street. Do you want to see him?"

"Yes," she replied softly.

"Yes," I echoed into the receiver.

"I'll be right over."

While we waited for Father O'Brien, Karen and I sat on the beds and talked about the last thirteen hours. I couldn't help myself repeating Dr. Hecht's comments about the baby "hanging in" and what a "fighter" she was, in part to try and counteract what Karen had just seen with her own eyes. I wanted to help boost her hope, despite what we'd witnessed and been told.

Karen listened quietly, nodding occasionally. At the end of my recital, she sat silently for a few more seconds. Then she said, "I think we should give the baby a name."

My spirit soared at those words, but I didn't want her doing this just for me. "Are you sure?" I asked.

Karen was still visibly weak, but her words were firm. "Yes. At the very least—no matter what happens—we owe her a name."

Before this we had been discussing names and reading through baby-name books. If the baby was a boy we were leaning toward Paul, but if it was a girl, Dana was our top choice. We had also talked about Victoria or Jocelyn as possible middle names. These choices were based, for the most part, simply on the fact that we liked the way they sounded.

"What are you thinking about for a name?" I asked.

Karen didn't hesitate. "Faith," she replied.

Faith! Electricity shot through me. We had considered the names Hope and Faith back when Karen had first been pregnant in Saudi Arabia, simply because they sounded nice to us, along with the desirable connotations of character and virtue they suggested. But now!

I was in awe. "That's great," I said. It was such a brave and perfect choice.

Our conversation was interrupted by a polite knock. Standing in the open doorway was a slim, young, dark-haired guy. Maybe because I was seated, I noticed his shoes first. They were black, highly polished, and stylish. "I'm Father O'Brien," he said.

When I had heard the name Father O'Brien and spoken to him on the phone, I had pictured an old Irish priest, white-haired, wrinkled, warm and wise like in Spencer Tracy movies. Not a young, hip guy.

He sat down in the one chair and we sat on the beds. He folded his hands in his lap and leaned forward. He did not appear sad or nervous. Just interested and calm. "So. You have a little baby. You want to tell me about it?"

Karen looked to me. I tried to keep my voice steady as I told him about the baby's poor prognosis and the many difficulties she faced. I found myself up on my feet. It was exciting and somehow freeing to share our situation so completely with someone else. He listened and nodded. Karen chimed in, helping to recount all the details.

At the end of our story, he asked, "Does the baby have a name?"

Karen and I looked at each other and in unison answered, "Faith." It felt strange to say it out loud.

Father O'Brien nodded, not showing any reaction. "Is there a middle name?" he asked.

Karen answered, "Can you tell us the names of any strong saints?"

In the Catholic tradition, it's common to name children after a saint of the church. We had named our son Andrew because the Apostle Andrew was one of the first to follow Jesus, and he was also the patron saint of Scotland, where we had lived and taught for three years, and Russia, where many of my ancestors were from. I always felt instinctively that names could be powerful. We could absolutely use a powerful name right now.

Father O'Brien said, "Well, there's Victoria—and Catherine.

They come to mind." He told us first about Victoria, but we quickly forgot all about her as he continued, "Then Saint Catherine of Siena. She was a mother, scholar, and diplomat. She was strong and wise. She advised kings and world leaders and was known for her diplomacy and ability to expertly weigh and balance the issues that faced her as well as the many roles she filled in life."

Karen and I looked at each other again when he mentioned the word *balance*. Dr. Hecht had repeatedly emphasized the delicate balance in play, between too much oxygen and too little, between necessary intervention and infection risk, of the electrolyte balance in the baby's blood. Balance was a key to our daughter's survival.

We agreed instantly. The baby's name would be Faith Catherine. Then Karen shifted gears. She asked Father O'Brien, "Do you know the book *When Bad Things Happen to Good People*?"

In the early eighties, it was a worldwide bestseller. We'd both read it when we were in Scotland and discussed it a lot. The author, Harold Kushner, a rabbi, tries to reason why if there is a good, kind, loving God there is still so much evil and pain in the world.

Father O'Brien nodded. "Yes. I'm familiar with it."

Karen said, "When I first read it, it seemed reasonable. God not being able to control everything helped explain why there is so much evil in the world, and like the title, why so many bad things happen to good people. But it went against what I learned in the church growing up."

"Which is?" Father O'Brien asked.

If there was ever a time to talk about these issues, it was now, and I was glad Karen was doing it. She spoke pointedly to Father

O'Brien. "That God does control everything. Kushner says that God is good and loving and will give us strength to endure trials we encounter, but that He doesn't control everything. If that's true, then maybe God can't control this."

Father O'Brien answered evenly, "Well, God will always listen to a parent praying for a child."

Karen simply nodded. I could tell from her expression that she felt the answer sidestepped her question, but that she didn't want to press him. Then Father O'Brien asked, "Would you want to pray together?"

"Sure. Yes," I said quickly. I was glad to have a "professional" there to lead us in prayer.

He gestured for us to stand with him. "Let's join hands," he said.

I hesitated. This was not normal prayer procedure for me. I thought we would sit where we were, bow our heads, he would say a prayer, and Karen and I would say "Amen" and that would be that.

Instead we all stood. He reached out and took our hands and we formed a circle. This was *really* different. The door was wide open and we were right in front of it. Anyone passing by could see and hear us. Father O'Brien closed his eyes and prayed loudly, "Dear Lord Jesus Christ, we ask you now to help Faith Catherine. We ask you for a miracle. We know you have done them before and we ask you for one now."

Suddenly, I was crying. How incredibly bold to ask God for a miracle. *Out loud!* Father O'Brien used that very word, *miracle.*

Everything I had ever asked God for had been private. If my prayer wasn't answered, that was just for me to know. I had certainly never asked out loud for a miracle.

And just like that, a dark stain began to seep in all over my shiny white hope. Hadn't we already been told by the medical experts more than once that the baby basically had no chance? Yes, she was hanging on, but it hadn't even been twenty-four hours. She was being kept alive by machines. And Karen and I just had the audacity to name our baby, of all things, Faith in the face of her imminent death. Naming a baby Faith, publicly praying for a miracle, and then having her die? What would that mean? That God isn't always able to control these things? Or worse, that He is not real and our faith is just a childish fantasy? I was frightened by where we had ventured.

Then my seesawing brain tipped again in the other direction. I *had* to believe that God could and would answer our prayer. Hadn't He already given us the three little miracles? And a priest to push us on. I had to believe He could do this. He would do this.

Father O'Brien finished the prayer and we all said "Amen." Wiping tears from our eyes, we thanked him and walked with him out into the hall. It no longer seemed like the right time to ask about funerals and last rites. Not after what we had just prayed for.

Karen had walked back to her bed and was seated on the edge. "I'm going to lie down," she said.

I went over, tucked her in, and kissed her. "Good. Get some rest."

I headed for the door. There was something I had to do.

CHAPTER 10

Viable

Walking quickly back down the hall to the NICU, I washed my hands in the little scrub room, tied on a gown, and went straight in. There were new nurses at the warmer and no Dr. Hecht. They somehow seemed to know who I was though, and greeted me with a chorus of hellos.

I glanced down at the baby and my breath caught again. She was so thin. Her arms and legs were literally like sticks, as thick as my finger. I looked up and addressed the nurses. "I wanted to let you know we named the baby." I paused. I wasn't sure who you were supposed to tell, but they nodded and smiled in what I took for encouragement, so I kept going. "Her name is Faith."

One nurse remarked, "Oh, how pretty."

"That is nice," said another.

Then I shared my mission. "I'd like to baptize her again. If that's okay."

There was no hesitation. "Sure. Certainly," they said.

One nurse walked over to a nearby counter, coming back a second later with another small bottle of sterilized water. I unscrewed the cap and lightly dipped a thumb in. As the baby twitched and strained, I reached in and gently traced the sign of the cross on her tiny forehead. *"Faith Catherine, I baptize you* in the name of the Father, and of the Son, and of the Holy Spirit. Amen."

A nurse picked up a marker and promptly wrote in bold, black letters across the top of the pink-and-blue identification card—*FAITH KRECH*. It finally felt complete.

I handed the water back and stood by. I glanced up at the wall clock. 9:15 a.m. About eight hours to go to hit the twenty-four-hour mark. "Mr. Krech," a nurse said.

I turned. "Yes?"

Standing there next to the nurse was a compact woman in sharply pressed blue scrubs. She was not much more than five feet tall with brown skin and dark hair pulled back. She wore a white surgical mask, the first one I had seen on anyone in the NICU. "This is Dr. Aragones," the nurse said. "Another of our neonatologists."

Dr. Aragones shook hands demurely and nodded a greeting. "I have seen your baby." Her voice was quiet, muffled by the mask. She spoke with a heavy accent, which sounded Filipino to me.

Unfortunately, I'd had a few bad experiences with a couple of Filipino doctors while living in Saudi Arabia, not to mention the one with Karen here at Mercer. They were, in my estimation, less knowledgeable than their American counterparts. It was an unfair generalization and I knew that, but I felt it nonetheless. I wished Dr. Hecht were still on duty. Last night I'd wanted to leap across a hospital bed and shake the woman and now here I was missing her.

At six foot one, I had to lean in and down to hear Dr. Aragones. She noticed this and lowered her mask in response, speaking slowly as she shared her observations. "Mr. Krech, your daughter is very sick. As you know, she is critical. She has a very poor prognosis."

It felt like she was obligated to say these things. Like a legal disclaimer. Even so, it was still scary to hear them. She paused and I responded, "Yes. I'm aware."

Dr. Aragones continued somberly, "She is requiring a great deal of oxygen. Unfortunately, her electrolyte balance has been up and down. Her blood gas tests are not as good as they had been."

My stomach sank. Dr. Aragones consulted her clipboard. "We have also received the results of an ultrasound taken of the baby's brain, which reveals a small, grade-one bleed."

A brain bleed!

Dr. Aragones paused again, watching me. I nodded and she continued, "It appears old, maybe from in the womb, but this is very common in preemies." Then she quickly explained, "The circulatory system of these infants is so immature and delicate that it is easy for blood vessel walls to give way under the strain and stress of being out of the womb. A bleed can cause loss of brain function and result in various disabilities like cerebral palsy, retardation, and others."

She moved her small hands delicately as she spoke. "Fortunately, the baby's bleed at this point is minor. Hopefully it will resolve itself and she will not have any more of them."

I stood quietly, taking all this in, thinking about how even if the baby survived now, with a brain bleed she could be...

"You understand, of course, that because of her low birth weight, there are other difficulties and risks we must manage." I nodded my understanding again. "Still," she said, "we will try."

"*Still, we will try?*" I wanted to say very directly. "*No! Just trying is not good enough. Save her!*" But I just stayed quiet and nodded.

She paused briefly. "The first seventy-two hours are very important. If a child can survive these first seventy-two hours, then we would consider her to be viable."

She didn't even mention the twenty-four-hour mark. I looked down into the warmer. The baby's legs were trembling. Her eyes were still fused shut. I wanted to tell her, "Come on, Faith. You can make seventy-two hours."

And then it hit me. I had thought of her as *Faith*. It was the first time. She was *Faith Krech*.

I thanked Dr. Aragones and she moved on. I remained by the warmer. Dr. Aragones had seemed very negative. Very pessimistic. And she was Filipino. All of this was unsettling. One of the nurses began to adjust the wires attached to the baby's chest.

I asked her, "Have you worked with Dr. Aragones long?" I was hoping to get some reassurance. Like maybe she was going to tell me how Dr. Aragones was the best doctor ever.

She shook her head. "No. She's new to the hospital."

"Really?"

"Yes. She works for a medical services company in Florida. She and another neonatologist come up to staff the unit for a couple of weeks at a time. Weekends and nights, we have Dr. Hecht and some other doctors."

I was thinking, oh my God, it's like Rent-a-Doctor, when another nurse, maybe fifteen feet away, walked up to Dr. Aragones and asked a question I couldn't hear. When Dr. Aragones replied, the nurse repeated the name of a drug questioningly.

Dr. Aragones calmly answered, "Yes. That is correct. Two cc's."

The nurse shrugged and as she walked away said loudly and deliberately for everyone in the room to hear, "Well, I've never done *that* before."

It was perfect timing.

CHAPTER 11

Asking to Fly

Unsure of what to say, ask, or do next, I just stood there watching Dr. Aragones walk away without a glance back at the nurse. I wondered if we had any choice as to who Faith's neonatologist would be. I was about to leave and try to regroup when a nurse in pastel green scrubs strolled over and thrust out a thin hand. She had a halo of dark, wiry hair framing a kind face and a huge smile. "Hi, I'm Suzie. I'm Faith's nurse this shift."

We shook hands. "I didn't realize she had her own nurse."

Suzie chuckled. "Yep. Even though it always looks like there's a crowd, we're assigned one-on-one with her. Of course, everyone pitches in."

She shifted the tiny water bed. "You know, your girl doesn't like lying on her belly." Suzie bent down and ran her finger along Faith's arm. "No, you don't. You get fussy. And you're always antsy after a pee, aren't you?"

Then in a confidential tone, she said, "She doesn't like a wet diaper. She doesn't like her blood drawn either."

"Wow. You know all this already?" It was a welcome change to hear about mundane things like wet diapers instead of oxygen levels and brain bleeds.

"Oh yeah," she said nonchalantly. "We get to know them pretty well since it's all one-on-one. Plus, each nurse writes up notes after every shift for the next nurse." She held up a thick black three-ring binder with Faith's name on the cover.

I wanted to ask this kind, gentle person who already knew our baby so well, I longed to ask her honestly, "Will she live though?" Instead, I pointed to a pad underneath Faith. "Is that the diaper?"

She laughed in reply. "Yeah. She's still too small for a regular diaper, even the preemie size, so we cut our smallest preemie diaper in half and have her lie on it." Suzie slid the diaper out from under Faith. "We weigh each of these before we dispose of them to check the amount of urine she's passed. It's one way to monitor her systems."

Suzie's smiling, upbeat work with Faith was a welcome contrast to Dr. Aragones's somber pronouncements. "Thanks, Suzie," I said.

"No problem. Come back anytime. We'll be here," she said jauntily.

I headed off to Karen's room. She was in bed, but awake. I told her about meeting Suzie and Dr. Aragones. She promptly sat up. "I'd like to try and see her again. This afternoon."

"Sounds good," I said in what I hoped was an encouraging tone. I was glad to hear she was up for it after yesterday.

The next couple of hours, I sat and read the preemie literature from Dr. Hecht while Karen dozed on and off. I considered going back into the NICU, but I didn't want to stand there just watching. I wanted to do something that might potentially be helpful, like learning more about what was going on.

Two of the pamphlets had the same title: *Your Special Newborn*. The third was *BPD: A Parent Guide to Bronchopulmonary Dysplasia*. So many bad things affected preemies, and they were all described in detail here. Still, I wanted to be prepared so I read on.

After lunch in the room, Karen brushed her hair and got into the wheelchair. I brought her down to the NICU and through that same door for her second visit. We scrubbed up quietly and got our gowns on, helping each other tie the backs closed. I was hoping there would be something we would see that would encourage Karen. As we entered and approached the warmer, a small nurse with shiny, light brown skin and dark eyes came forward and greeted us, introducing herself as Meera.

She spoke with a lovely Indian accent and cadence. "Your daughter is doing very, very good, you know. She is quite a fighter." She looked down and wiggled a finger at Faith. "Aren't you, little girl?"

Wait. What? *She was doing good? Very good?*

Meera turned to Karen, bent down, and took both her hands. "Here. Come up here, Mommy. Let me help you. You can see her." Meera and I supported Karen as she stood and peered into the warmer for the second time.

"Go ahead. You can touch her," Meera urged.

Faith lay there on her back, twitching and trembling. Karen reached out a finger and tentatively touched her arm. Then she sat back down, wiping her eyes, but smiling. "Thank you," Karen said.

"That's fine," Meera replied, nodding encouragement. "Anytime you want to see her, you just come right in."

We thanked Meera, and I wheeled Karen back to the room. When we got there, she lay down on the bed and looked across at me. In a quiet, awed voice she said, "She's so tiny. So fragile. I've never seen anything like her before."

That was the truth. Her size was just—incredible.

I honestly did not feel the same connection I had with Andrew as a newborn. I felt bad about it, but I couldn't deny it was true. I had touched Faith only twice with the tip of my finger when I baptized her. Not since. Pretty much all I was doing was watching her. The only other thing I could think to do was ask questions and learn as much as I could. Mostly I was just there.

I went back to the NICU and watched Meera in action for another hour that afternoon while Karen slept. I noticed that Meera was constantly turning Faith's oxygen percentage and rate up and down. She administered medications through the long tube in Faith's navel and supervised people who came and took blood. Faith jerked and twitched through it all. It was unsettling to watch, but the very good news was—she was still hanging in there. And Meera kept reiterating how "very, very good" Faith was doing.

Around four o'clock I went back to Karen's room. She was asleep, so I sat on the other bed and took out the literature on premature infants again. I finished reading after another hour. It looked like everything that was mentioned in the pamphlets, they were doing to Faith. I glanced up at the clock. It was just about 5:00 p.m. We were almost there.

I studied the small color photos of the babies in the incubators and the detailed medical descriptions. It still seemed like someone else's life I was reading about. Then I allowed myself another peek. 5:21. I looked away and closed my eyes. One more minute. When I looked back, it was 5:22. No calls from the NICU. No nurses rushing down the hall. Somehow Faith had made it twenty-four hours.

I felt a need to go thank God immediately and personally. I went out into the hall and asked the first nurse I saw, "Could you tell me where the hospital chapel is?"

It turned out that it was on the ground floor near the front entrance. I pushed through the heavy wooden doors and entered the hush of a small, dimly lit, empty room. It was about the size of our family room at home. Two brightly colored stained-glass windows framed the altar. A large Bible sat in a wooden stand on one corner of the altar. Four rows of simple wood pews ran on each side of a center aisle.

The thick wooden doors closed gently behind me. I knelt in a pew and prayed sincerely, *Thank you, God, for Faith's twenty-four hours. Please help her. Please keep her alive. Please save her.*

Considering all I'd seen, all I'd read, and all I'd been told by these doctors, it felt like asking to fly.

CHAPTER 12

Not a Good Morning

I returned to the room and Karen woke up a little later. We ate our dinners on trays as the sun set. I could see she was still weak, but I wanted to stay open to her joining me again whenever she was ready. After we finished, I asked, "Do you want to go back over and see her?"

"Yes," Karen said immediately. There was that determination again in the way she voiced that one word.

"Should I get the wheelchair?"

"No," she said, standing. "I'll walk."

We made our way arm in arm down the hall and back into the NICU. I got a reassuring feeling when I saw that Meera was still there to greet us. She put a welcoming arm around Karen. "Oh good. You're here," she said warmly. "Faith is going to have her weigh-in at seven o'clock."

No mention of the twenty-four-hour mark. I figured I wouldn't either. I was also surprised that they were bothering to weigh a child who was so critical. I asked Meera, "So is weighing her important?"

She replied, "Gaining weight is very important. Weight gain strengthens them and makes them more resistant to infection."

Maybe we were about to see a significant weight gain up from the 450 grams she weighed at birth. Maybe another little miracle. I was also wondering how you weigh someone so small. As if in answer to my question, two nurses approached us wheeling a cart. On top was a small electronic scale. "Here they are," Meera said brightly.

One of the nurses covered the scale with a thin blue blanket. The other bent over the warmer and said, "Ready for a weigh-in, little missy?" She reached down and put her hands under Faith's tiny head and bottom. "We have everything?" the nurse with Faith asked.

The nurse with the scale nodded. "Yep. Let's go." She counted, "One, two—three."

Meera joined in the lift, and they swept Faith up out of the warmer and onto the scale in one smooth move. Then, just as quickly, she was whisked off and back into the warmer. The scale's digital readout flashed red—430 grams.

Faith had *lost twenty grams*. The three nurses exchanged glances. One of them said, "That's probably not right. Let's try it again."

We waited quietly as the erroneous readout cleared. Again, the tiny body was hoisted in the air, carefully placed on the scale, and returned gently to the warmer. A pause. The red digits glared back—430 grams.

Then Meera took charge of the situation. She brought her brown, shining face close to Faith's and wagged a finger at her as she scolded, "You will have to cut back on those Jane Fonda tapes, little girl."

I grinned involuntarily. For a moment, the tension was broken. Meera turned to Karen and me and dismissed the whole thing with a careless shake of her head. "They always lose weight right after birth. It's nothing. Normal babies do this as well. You two know that."

Karen agreed, saying, "That's true. Andrew did."

Of course, Andrew had weighed 8 pounds and 6 ounces when he was born, but I wasn't going to mention that right now.

We stood there for a moment trying to regain our equilibrium while the nurses carried on around us. Karen looked to me. "I think I'm ready to go," she said quietly.

As we walked together back to her room, we passed a waiting area where *Monday Night Football* flashed across a TV screen. Again, I had zero interest. The world out there was completely irrelevant.

Back in the room, Karen sank into her bed and closed her eyes. She was soon asleep. I sat in the chair and began studying the prematurity and neonatal-care brochures again.

As the night went on, I maintained my three-hour visiting intervals. I couldn't sleep well, so it was no big effort to get up out of bed, walk a few yards down the hall, and check things out. Dr. Hecht was back on duty. She didn't comment on me being there in the middle of the night. She just filled me in. "She's still critical. No real breathing on her own yet. Her blood gases are not that good either, but Bob—she's hanging in."

"That's great." It was so good to see Dr. Hecht back with Faith and to hear her use my first name. A gap had closed between us.

"Yes, but we want to get her off that respirator as soon as we can." Dr. Hecht gave a small sigh. "Hopefully in the next week or two. She has to start assisting though."

I brightened. Dr. Hecht had said "the next week or two." She was talking about the future.

•••

I returned from my final visit of the night at 6:00 a.m. It was now Tuesday morning, November 10. Back in the room, Karen was already awake. We hugged as I filled her in. A young nurse appeared at the door with breakfast. "Good morning," she said brightly.

Karen pulled herself up in bed. "Good morning."

The nurse put the tray down and adjusted the bed. "You're going to be able to go home this morning, Karen. Dr. Baumann signed your discharge papers already."

Karen's face registered surprise. "Oh. Okay," she replied.

I hadn't thought about us leaving the hospital either. It was like, if the baby was there, we should be too.

Karen ate and got dressed. It took only a couple of minutes to pack up her few things and we were out. We did not stop back at the NICU to see Faith before we left. Karen didn't ask to and I had just seen her.

The drive home was a strange mix of long, thoughtful silences punctuated by bursts of intense discussion. "I'll be so glad to see Andrew an hold him," Karen said more than once.

It felt good to open the front door and step back into our house. To be home. The softer colors of the walls and the warm brown wood floor were a welcome change after the sterile grays and blues of the hospital. A feeling of normalcy and quiet enveloped us.

Within minutes, however, the phone began ringing. Two white vans arrived back-to-back delivering flowers and plants. Word had spread. No matter where we were now, hospital or home, things were never going back to the way they were.

Karen walked through the rooms downstairs. She embraced me. She was crying again. "Every time I think about Faith, I well up," she whispered.

"I know. Me too."

"All these flowers and the plants... I don't know..."

"Yeah." It made me think about sick people and funerals, but I wasn't going to say that out loud.

"Let's ask your parents to bring Andrew home," she said.

I went upstairs, called my parents, then checked our messages. Most were from friends and relatives expressing their concern and asking us to call and let them know what was going on.

The third message on the machine, though, was from Scott Questad, a guy I knew mainly through his wife, Ceil, a colleague at work. I heard the beep and then Scott's hearty, upbeat voice: "Hello, Kreches! Congratulations on the new baby and good luck with everything."

Congratulations? No one had used that word yet. He was also the only man to call. I didn't know Scott well, but people who did often described him as a "really religious guy" or "strong Christian." Was that why his phone message was so different?

We returned a few calls and then my parents pulled into the drive with Andrew. He came running up the walk, arms full of grandparent-bought goodies.

"Hey, buddy, how are you doing?" I hugged him.

"Great," he said jauntily. "How are you doing?"

"Okay, pal." Just seeing him made me smile.

Karen scooped him up and pressed him tight to her chest. We went inside and shared all the latest details with my mom and dad.

After we caught up, I walked them to the door. My mother said, "If you need anything, you just let us know." She didn't have to say it. That's just how it was in our family.

Meanwhile, I had already started to worry about how things were going back at the hospital. Dr. Hecht had made a point of letting us know that we had twenty-four-hour access to the unit. We could call at any time and they would update us.

So I called. Just to test the system. We already knew pretty much how things stood. It had only been two hours since we left.

A nurse answered, "NICU. This is Katie."

"Hi, this is Bob Krech. I'm calling to check on my daughter, Faith Krech."

"I'll get Dr. Aragones for you," she replied.

I waited for what seemed like a long time. Finally, a small, muffled voice came on, made even softer and more foreign by the phone. "Yes, Mr. Krech."

"Hi, Dr. Aragones. I'm just calling to see how Faith is doing."

There was a brief pause. "Well...she is not having a very good morning."

CHAPTER 13

Nowhere to Turn

O h my God, I thought. What does that mean?

Before I could ask the question out loud, Dr. Aragones explained. "Her potassium is high. And we have not been able to bring it down yet." She paused. "I am going to give her a barium enema, which will hopefully help draw it out of her."

"So it's just too much potassium in her blood?" I strained to hear the small voice answer.

"Well," she explained carefully, "if there is too much potassium in the blood, heart failure can result. Unless we can reverse this, we could lose her very quickly."

I sank down on the arm of the couch. I answered automatically. "I see."

Her soft, muffled voice drifted up to me again across the phone lines. "Still, we will try."

Again "we will try." I wanted to shout, *"Don't just try. Just trying is not good enough. Keep her alive!"* Instead, I said, "Thank you, Doctor."

I hung up. Karen stood in place staring at me, waiting. I repeated Dr. Aragones's message. We hugged and held again. My next thought was to get right back to the hospital, but what would that accomplish? That, and what would I be running back to?

Karen returned to holding Andrew. I climbed the stairs to our bedroom and knelt down by the bed to pray. I did not know what else to do.

I cried and prayed. I don't know how long I knelt there. It might have been ten minutes. It could have been an hour. *Lord, please help Faith get to the seventy-two-hour mark. Please let her live.* I prayed this over and over again like a mantra.

Eventually, I got up and sat on the edge of the bed. I was hoping that my prayers would give me a feeling of reassurance. Some confidence. Instead, I had the same chilling fear in my gut. Faith was in dire trouble.

But what else was there to do? I had nowhere to turn except to God, and I was praying constantly and more intensely than I ever had in my life. I walked to the window and looked out into the backyard.

I had always had control over my life. That was what I thought anyway. I'd wanted to get a teaching job right out of college, when there were no jobs, and I'd gotten one. I'd wanted to live and work overseas and make good money as a teacher. I'd made it happen. I'd wanted us to travel, get a nice house, start a family. It had all happened. Even when we were in Saudi Arabia and Karen had had two miscarriages, I'd known we could find the right doctor, find the right solution to the problem, and we had. But this... I had no answers.

Ask and ye shall receive.

Those five words just floated into my consciousness right then.

Ask and ye shall receive.

I wasn't trying to think of verses, or passages, or scripture, but suddenly the words were in my mind.

Ask and ye shall receive.

And then, right on top of that, a second phrase emerged. *Have faith like a mustard seed.*

Now, I had *never* memorized any Bible passages, ever. I didn't even read the Bible. But I must have heard these two verses read to me enough times in church that they stuck somewhere. And now here they were. Unbidden. It's not like I heard a voice or anything, but these distinct phrases suddenly just emerged in my consciousness. I don't know how else to describe it.

I felt instinctively that this was important and that I should do something about it. But what? I figured they had to be from the Bible somewhere, so I reached in my night-table drawer and pulled out our one Bible. It was a small paperback with tiny print, the kind you would find in a hotel room. I had never read it. I kept it more as a symbol of faith, like a cross on the wall.

I flipped back and forth through flimsy, densely printed pages, not even knowing where to begin looking. I wanted to find these words, to know more, but after twenty minutes of frantic searching, I was getting nowhere.

Normally, I would be far too self-conscious to call someone to ask if they could help me do something like find a Bible verse, or I could wait till next Sunday at church—and how was that going to help anyway?—but I was way past that sort of reticence. Anything I could do to help Faith, I would do it and now. And somehow, I believed this would help.

I picked up the phone by the bed and called Melanie Faulkner. Melanie was a first-grade teacher in my school whose husband, Greg, was a divinity student at nearby Princeton Theological Seminary. I was sure Greg would know where to find the passages. Melanie was surprised to hear from me, but I quickly filled her in about the baby. She immediately asked, "How can I help?"

It was a weird request, but it was what I needed. "Well, I need to find out where a couple of Bible verses are from."

"Oh. Which ones?"

"Well, one is about ask and ye shall receive, and the other is something about having the faith of a mustard seed. Would you know?"

"I will certainly find out from Greg and I'll call you right back."

Fifteen minutes later the phone rang. "Hey, Bob. I got your verses. The first is in Matthew, chapter seven, verses seven and eight. The second one is Matthew also, chapter seventeen, verse twenty."

I jotted this down and said, "Thanks, Mel. And thank Greg for me, please."

"No problem," she said. "We'll be praying for you."

Growing up in my local Catholic church, there was no Bible study. You went to church and heard Bible passages read to you and you read along in the missal. You went to religious instruction where most of the focus was on memorizing lists like the Ten Commandments and prayers like the Act of Contrition. Nobody I knew studied the Bible or even read it outside of church. The first person I ever met who did anything like that was Gary, a guy on my dorm floor freshman year at Rutgers.

I was eighteen years old and my priorities were sleeping as late as I could, trying to meet cute girls, playing basketball as much as possible, and getting on the dean's list. Meanwhile, Gary had already served two years in the air force and was running a five-mile loop around the campus every morning at dawn, repeating Bible verses he was committing to memory as he ran. He had them written neatly on index cards, tucked in his shirt pocket, and he carried them everywhere. I thought this was all a little overboard.

I remembered hearing once in church about "hungering for God's Word," and now, for the first time ever, I actually felt that. I literally craved these verses more than food.

I leafed through the pages till I found Matthew 7:7–8. I skimmed it quickly to be sure it was the right one, then read it again more deliberately: "Ask, and it will be given to you; seek, and you will find; knock, and it will be opened to you. For everyone who asks receives, and he who seeks finds, and to him who knocks it will be opened."

I immediately loved the fact that these were Jesus's own words. It sounded to me like He was saying to ask *Him* for help when I needed it. But more importantly, it went on to say, "*Ask, and it will be given to you.*"

Not just ask, but expect to get what you ask for.

Did I believe this? I honestly didn't know. Again, like with Father O'Brien, I was scared and hesitant because I thought if this didn't work, it would mean that God did not honor His promises, or worse, that He was not really even there.

I went on to the next verse, Matthew 17:20. Jesus is answering His disciples, who have asked Him why they could not cure an epileptic boy brought to them by the boy's distraught father.

Jesus answers, "Because of your unbelief, for assuredly, I say to you, if you have faith as a mustard seed, you will say to this mountain, 'Move from here to there,' and it will move; and nothing will be impossible for you."

We had already asked for the impossible with Father O'Brien.

"Nothing will be impossible for you," Jesus said.

Obviously, I'd heard these verses enough times to leave an impression. Now, however, they were shouting at me. *"Ask! And you will receive! Nothing will be impossible for you."*

I seized the verses like a drowning man tossed a life preserver. I sank to my knees. It was time to pray again. *Lord, you told us to ask and we would receive. You told us to have faith, even as small as a mustard seed, and we would be able to move mountains. That nothing is impossible. Please help Faith to live. Please use her nurses, and her doctors. Guide them to make the right decisions so she might live. Thank you. Amen.*

I felt like I had somehow stumbled upon, or maybe been led to, the right thing to do. The right tool. I was doing something I had never done before. I was claiming promises from God. My logic, if you could call it that, was simple. I believed in God. I believed in His Word. I believed in His promises.

And it was all about to be tested.

CHAPTER 14

Hanging In

I went back downstairs. Karen was on the couch in the family room, Andrew curled up contentedly on her lap. A sweet, peaceful scene I was about to break up. "Karen, do you want to go back this afternoon?" I asked.

A worried look spread across her face, and just as quickly faded. She nodded. "Yes. We should."

It would have been easier for us to stay right here at home with Andrew, but we were compelled. We had to be there for Faith.

That afternoon we brought Andrew back to my parents' house. He scampered happily up their driveway, oblivious to the events swirling around him while Karen and I drove back to Mercer.

We walked into the NICU scrub room. It had become a buffer zone of sorts for me. I prepared myself not only physically by washing my hands and putting on a gown, but mentally as well. Have faith as a mustard seed. Ask and you will receive. I was asking. Please let her be okay in there. Peeking through the window, my stomach in a knot, I saw there was only one nurse next to Faith's warmer. I took that as a good sign. I pushed open the door and Karen and I were once again engulfed by the sounds of beeping alarms, humming machinery, the squeak of nurses' sneakers across the linoleum. It reminded me that this was not a nursery. It was an intensive care unit. My pulse quickened.

I hadn't met the nurse by the warmer. She was a short young woman with a long brown ponytail. She introduced herself as Cindy. "How is Faith?" I asked.

In a neutral voice she said, "Well, about the same. No real changes." Then she added quickly, "Which is good."

Lying in the metal tray under the bright white light, Faith did look exactly the same. Strips of tape ran across her face in an X, holding her breathing tube in her mouth. Her twig-like arms and legs twitched jerkily, as if she had no control over them. Could these spastic movements mean some kind of neurological damage?

I nodded to Cindy, then asked cautiously, "I understand she had some problems this morning."

She paused. "Yes, her potassium is still high. It's too early to say what effect the barium enema will have."

"How's everything else?" I was hoping for something positive to cling to.

She replied, "Well, her blood gas was not as good as previously, and she isn't assisting the respirator yet, but she is hanging in." Then with a note of admiration she added, "She's tough."

I liked hearing that, but as Karen and I stood there helplessly watching this tiny infant twist and turn, it still honestly did not look good. After less than an hour we headed home, picking Andrew up on our way. We cooked dinner together and sat down to eat when the phone rang. We exchanged a frightened glance. Now I was scared of the phone.

I answered and the woman on the other end said, "Hi, Mr. Krech? I'm Lauri Davison. Dr. Baumann asked that I call you and share some things with you. You see, I had a preemie at Mercer too." I thanked her and passed the phone on to Karen. The young mom on the other end told Karen about her experience with her premature son in the NICU and how he was now three years old and doing very well. This was encouraging, to an extent.

The problem was that her son was 3 pounds when he was born. Just like in all the pamphlets I'd been reading, every premature baby, without exception, was significantly bigger and older than Faith at birth. This point was hammered home again later that night.

We returned to the NICU immediately after dinner. When we got there, we found four nurses tightly packed around Faith's warmer. They looked like they were working intensely, so Karen and I moved off to the side. I hoped that this many people didn't mean something worse was happening.

As we stood there, I noticed a chart on the wall. It was a preemie weight chart showing conversions from pounds and ounces to kilograms and grams. I looked for Faith's weight, 450 grams. The chart *began* at 500 grams. Faith wasn't even close to being on a *preemie* weight chart.

Soon the group of nurses moved on except for one. Karen asked her, "How is she?"

The nurse hesitated, then answered, "Oh, stable. Hanging in."

"That's good," Karen replied.

"Oh yes," she said. "Stable is very good."

She was a young nurse and appeared nervous, but I had to ask. "Excuse me. I was just wondering, how does Faith compare with other preemies you've worked with? Have you had other babies like her?" I asked hopefully.

"Well," she said in a purposeful, offhand manner, "she's the smallest and youngest ever born at this hospital to survive this long."

This was new territory for these doctors and nurses too. It made me think about Dr. Aragones. It seemed that Faith's condition had deteriorated soon after she came on in the morning. I wondered how much she would be involved in Faith's care and if it was time to think about moving Faith to another hospital, like Children's in Philadelphia.

When we got home, I asked Karen, "Are you okay with me calling Tim Hall?" Tim was a heart surgeon in Princeton. We knew him socially through his wife and daughter, part of a playgroup Karen and Andrew belonged to.

"Yes," Karen said. "That's a good idea. It would be helpful to get his take on all this."

I wanted to find out if we were in the right place and doing everything we could.

I shared all the details on the phone with Tim that night. He asked questions that made it clear that although he was a heart surgeon and not a neonatologist, he knew exactly what was going on. I finally asked, "So, from what I've told you, is she in the right place?"

"Yes," he replied firmly. "Don't move her. They've done

everything they can, and they're very good. They're a level three regional perinatal center. You're not going to get better than them."

I was thankful for his firm answers and the lack of any equivocation.

"She's fine right where she is unless she needs special surgery," he continued. "If that happens, they'll probably take her down to Children's Hospital in Philadelphia. Also, be prepared, she's eventually going to get an infection. They all do, and if she can get past that, she should have a good chance."

"Thanks, Tim," I said.

"No problem," he replied. "Call me anytime. And good luck."

I hung up the phone and sat down at the kitchen table. Bits and pieces of my conversation with Tim ran through my mind. Tomorrow we would be closing in on the seventy-two-hour mark, God willing.

I smiled to myself about that little phrase—"God willing." I remembered how, when we were teaching in Saudi Arabia, every time we talked about something in the future—a trip somewhere, someone's health or job, even whether a plane would be on time— my Muslim acquaintances would always acknowledge that we could make our human plans, but it was ultimately up to God, "Inshallah." Arabic for "God willing."

I wrote out another set of sub plans for school, then went upstairs to bed. Karen was already fast asleep and I was so exhausted from my fear that I quickly fell into a heavy, deep sleep next to her. That's when I had the dream I would never forget.

CHAPTER 15

Seventy-Two Hours

This dream was unlike any I've ever had, before or since.

It was night and I was standing in the NICU next to Faith's warmer. The room was completely empty except for the two of us. She was lying there peaceful and quiet, not twitching and straining as usual. There was a cozy, calm feeling. Then I felt drawn to turn around.

When I did, I was facing the counter where the jar of water for Faith's baptism had been. The baptism with her name.

Standing next to the counter was a tall nurse with brown hair piled high on her head around an old-fashioned, white nurse's cap. She was looking directly at me. I got the clear impression that she wanted to tell me something, so I took a few steps toward her. It was like walking into a soft, warm cloud. When I was just a few feet away, I got the feeling that I should not come any closer. Even so, I was not scared. I felt comforted and safe in her presence.

She smiled slightly at me, then said clearly and kindly, "Faith is going to be all right."

A wave of relief washed over me. I felt so good. So content. I believed her completely. "Thank you," I said.

She smiled and dipped her head slightly, politely acknowledging my thanks as the dream faded.

When I woke up, I was still wrapped in that same feeling of warmth and comfort. I hadn't felt this good and rested in what seemed like a very long time. The thought went through my mind, could it have been an angel? An angel sent to reassure and comfort me? Or was it just my subconscious playing on my wishes?

I didn't tell anyone about the dream. Not even Karen. I didn't want to give her false hope, and I didn't want other people to start thinking I was losing it, like, "Oh, don't worry about Faith. I saw an angel in my dream who said everything was going to be fine." But the dream had delivered a deep comfort.

It was Wednesday morning, November 11. Today, God willing, Faith would be closing in on seventy-two hours. Still bathed in the warmth and good feelings from the dream, I called the school to arrange for a substitute teacher again and sent lesson plans in with Melanie. Karen and I decided to get to the hospital early, so my mother arrived to watch Andrew at our house. Driving in, fears about the potassium situation crept back into my mind. I tried to counter them with the reassurance from my dream. Yes, she was going to be all right.

As we entered the NICU, there was Suzie standing alone by Faith's warmer. It was an immediate boost to see her friendly face again. "Hey, look at Faith today," she called to us. Suzie had a big, easy smile and the enthusiasm of a preschool teacher. "She's started to open her eyes," she exclaimed.

I peered into the warmer. One eye was completely open and the other was starting. The open eye looked huge in that little face. It was bright blue. That's when I spotted a tiny plastic nipple lying near Faith's head. I blurted, "How did a nipple get in there?"

"It's never too early to try," Suzie said, grinning. "She's going to have to learn."

I couldn't help but grin back. Her positive outlook was contagious.

Suzie continued, "So—we've been talking as a staff about how this warmer tray is drying Faith out, even with the plastic-wrap cover. She's losing water weight, which she can't afford to do. We'd like to move her to an Isolette." She gestured toward one of the many clear, rectangular incubators that lined the walls. She gave a little sigh. "It would help to reduce the water weight loss, but it's just too early. She needs to be worked on too much yet."

Suzie pointed to Faith's abdomen. "The long line in Faith's navel was removed during the night. Now all of her nourishment and medication comes through an IV. That will cut down on the infection risk. On the downside, her veins are so weak and imma-ture that they tend to collapse after a little while as an IV site." She paused and shrugged. "But we keep a watch, and if it happens, we just find another site."

I couldn't imagine trying to find a *vein* on someone this small, and then managing to get a needle into it. Another nurse with curly dark hair and a wide, friendly face quickstepped over and extended her hand. "Hi, I'm Beth. It's nice to meet Faith's parents," she said.

Suzie said, "You know, Karen, if you don't mind my saying, probably the best thing you can do for Faith right now is to start pumping and freezing your breast milk."

Karen was visibly surprised. "Oh. Really?" she asked.

"Oh yeah," Beth agreed. "Breast milk is the best thing for Faith as soon as she can tolerate it. It's easy for her to digest, and it has all your antibodies to help build up her resistance. It can really help protect her."

Suzie chimed in, "It's liquid *gold*. Pump and freeze as much as you can, because it may not seem like it now, but she's going to need a lot of it down the line."

Karen and I exchanged a look and a small smile. Suzie and Beth kept using the future tense, and without any "ifs." It was like they were working with the assumption that Faith would just keep going.

Before we left, Beth handed Karen a small manual breast pump. She also gave her a pack of plastic baggies. "Here you go, Karen. Put your milk in these and mark them with Faith's name and the date. We'll put them in our freezer here and hold them till she's ready for them."

"Great. Thank you," Karen replied. You could see Karen was visibly pleased. The visit was so upbeat and positive that only when I was on the elevator did I remember about the potassium level.

After we got home and had lunch, Karen sat in a rocking chair in the bedroom. Eyes welling up, she started pumping milk for Faith.

I walked over and put an arm around her shoulder. "Are you sure you want to do this?" I asked.

She sniffed and nodded. "Yes. It's something I can do besides visit."

"Yeah. That's true," I replied. "It's good to be able to do something to help rather than just watch and listen."

"And you know..." She swallowed. "It cuts through the sadness somehow."

I thought it was a brave thing to do. I went out to Walmart and bought the smallest cooler I could find. There was one left. It just happened to be pink and white.

We went back to the hospital that afternoon with our cooler and three tiny packets of breast milk inside to find Meera on duty with Faith again. When Meera saw what Karen was holding, she practically cheered. "Oh, you have milk for her! That is so wonderful."

Karen turned red as Aunt Meera patted her shoulder and hugged her. Then Meera turned to me. "I have something for you too."

She reached into a shelf under Faith's warmer and pulled out a Polaroid camera. She thrust it at me. "You should take a picture of her," she urged.

I stood there very unsure. She pulled the plastic wrap back and waved me on. "Go ahead. You need a picture of your baby," she commanded.

I held the camera up and looked through the viewfinder. I'd never thought about taking a picture, and from the back of my mind another unwanted thought came forward. Did I want a picture of her if she was doing to die?

"She's so beautiful," another nurse chimed in.

With that, I pressed the button. The picture appeared a few

seconds later. It was a stark flash-lit image of a little body splayed out with tubes, wires, and tape. Meera peered over my shoulder. "Very good," she said. "Now you have a picture of her."

I passed it to Karen. She glanced at it and put it quickly in her purse. Meera took the camera and returned with two small tubes of cream. "Here. You know, this warmer is drying out her skin. You two can help keep her moist by putting this cream on her a couple of times a day," she said. "You just put a small dab on your fingertip and rub around all over gently." Meera demonstrated as she spoke. "Now here, you do it."

I was hesitant. "We won't be spreading any germs or anything to her?" I asked.

Meera shook her head. "No, no, no," she said. "Touching is a very good thing for her. The research shows that the more an infant is touched, especially by the parents, the faster they gain weight. So really they become stronger and more resistant to infections." She held her hand out with the tubes of cream. We each took one.

Karen put a small dab of the white cream on her fingertip, and then I did the same. Meera urged us on again. "Go ahead," she said. "You won't hurt her."

I moved my finger gently up her arm. The skin was thin, loose, and rubbery. I could feel the bone right underneath. Even so, it was good to be able to do something constructive for her. Then I remembered to ask about the potassium level, but I didn't do it. I didn't want to spoil all the positivity.

After the visit, Karen and I headed to my parents' house. We filled them in and picked Andrew up. We got home at about four o'clock and started dinner together. I watched the kitchen clock and prayed silently that the phone would not ring. I kept glancing up, mentally pushing those minutes forward. We were almost there.

Finally, mercifully, 5:22 p.m. came. *Seventy-two hours.* Faith had done it. In the parlance of the neonatologists, she was officially viable.

"She made it," I said. Karen and I hugged at the table while wiping away joyful tears.

Karen sighed. "Oh yes."

We stood there holding each other. Andrew rushed over to make it a group hug. We held hands and then began dancing around the kitchen in a circle, Andrew giggling, Karen and I singing nonsensically. Andrew had no idea why—but he was happy to join in.

•••

It was freezing out that night, but I barely noticed the cold on our way back to the NICU. I was flying. Faith had done it. She had made the seventy-two hours. She was going to be all right. Just like in my dream.

We walked in to find that Pam was Faith's nurse. Pam had been introduced to us briefly the day before. She was small with short, dark brown hair and a sturdy, compact body. She did not have a lot to say, not in a rude way, but she was just not a talker or big smiler. She had an air of quiet confidence about her though.

Karen and I stood by the warmer watching Pam with Faith. I was surprised that Pam hadn't mentioned the all-important seventy-two-hour mark, so I felt obliged to. As casually as I could, I said, "Well, she made it through seventy-two hours."

"Yep," Pam replied. Then completely deadpan, she added, "Now she's got like a thirty percent chance."

My heart plummeted to my stomach. I swallowed hard, then pushed the words out. "A thirty percent chance?"

Pam looked across the warmer at us and half smiled. "It's a lot better than the two percent she started with."

While we were digesting that, she looked to Karen and asked, "When was your due date again?"

Karen told her, "March sixth."

"Yeah," Pam said. "Well, you'll be with us all winter then."

Bounce! My heart was back up in its proper position. Maybe a little higher. Nothing gave me a greater charge than to hear these nurses talk about Faith in the future tense, especially someone as no-nonsense as Pam appeared to be.

The room had only one window to the outside. It was right near the counter where I had seen the nurse in my dream. While Pam and Karen talked, I walked to the window and looked out into the black night. Gazing down, I could see the little courtyard outside the chapel. A small amber light illuminated the stained-glass windows from within. Pam's words replayed in my mind: "You'll be with us all winter then."

I could easily picture snow falling gently into the courtyard below. I prayed silently that Pam was right. That it would not end before then. That we would all be there in the warmth of the NICU with our daughter, in the snow, in the winter.

CHAPTER 16

Back to School

To me, "viable" had meant *good, done, out, saved.* Now I knew it actually meant that Faith's chances of survival were about one in three.

Dr. Hecht's counseling us at Faith's birth, to keep her warm and let her pass on, was more and more understandable. She knew statistically, and probably from painful personal experience, that Faith's death was all but inevitable, and that our insistence on intervention would only be prolonging the baby's pain and our own, not to mention the staff, who would be futilely trying to save her.

But here we were. Seventy-two hours later. And she was still alive.

While most all of my focus was on Faith, I was still responsible for twenty-two second graders. On the way home, I told Karen, "I should probably go back to school tomorrow if you're okay with that. I can go to the hospital in the morning before work."

"That sounds fine," Karen replied. "I'll go in the afternoon."

"Yeah, we can go at night together," I said. "I feel like I should be at the hospital all the time, y'know?"

"I know." Karen nodded. "But we have to keep going on with our lives."

She was right, of course. Karen needed to be home during the day for Andrew, and I didn't want to leave my class with a substitute for too long. Kids can backslide very quickly academically and behaviorally. Besides, there was no real practical reason we had to be by Faith's side all throughout the day. It just felt like it.

Traffic was light in the early-morning dark on Thursday when I set out for the hospital. I got on the elevator, pressed 3, and my stomach automatically tensed. This was Day 5 for me in the NICU and it was still happening. I just had no idea what I would find each time. I said a silent prayer that all would be well.

From the scrub room window I could see there were two nurses near Faith. I went in and over to the warmer and said hi. Both women smiled. "Good morning," they said in unison.

As I peered into the tray, Faith appeared unusually still. She looked the same physically, but there was no wriggling and struggling. She just lay motionless. "How is she?" I asked tentatively.

One of the nurses answered. "Pretty stable."

"She seems real quiet," I offered.

The other nurse smiled again. "Yeah, she needed a little rest after all she's been through."

Before I could respond, a small, bent, older woman moved toward us, pushing a child-size shopping cart filled with racks of test tubes and vials.

"How's our little darling this morning?" she asked in a smoker's gravelly voice.

"Okay. This is Faith's dad," one of the nurses replied.

"Nice to meet you. I'm from the lab. We just need to get some blood." She climbed carefully onto a stool next to Faith's warmer. "Honey, it's Millie, and I need a little blood."

She glanced back. Deadpan, she said, "She hates this. She hates me."

Turning to Faith, she resumed. "I know, honey, this is not fun, but we need the blood." Then back to me. "I think she knows when I'm coming. She starts kicking before I even get near her."

Millie used a couple of thin, sharp pipettes to draw blood from Faith's heels. She dropped them into tubes and marked the labels. "I'll see you tomorrow, sweetheart," she said as she left.

A young guy in blue scrubs was waiting right behind her. "Good morning," he said. "I'm Jason. One of the respiratory technicians. Just checking the equipment and adding some medication."

Dr. Aragones appeared next. "Hello, Mr. Krech. Nice to see you," she said while leafing through her notes. "Faith is still in critical condition. But she is relatively stable."

Dr. Aragones didn't mention the potassium level. I assumed that was good news, but I didn't want to hear if it was otherwise, so I didn't bring it up. Hearing the word "stable" was good too. She stood there, maybe waiting for more questions from me, but I didn't know what else to ask.

As Dr. Aragones walked away, I had an impulse and reached in and lightly made the sign of the cross on Faith's forehead. A little blessing for the day.

I left the hospital, stopping at home for a quick breakfast with Karen. For the past two years, Karen had been at home full-time with Andrew. She resigned from her job teaching third grade when he was born and now taught English as a Second Language part-time to adults two nights a week in a community education program.

"How was she this morning?" Karen asked.

"The same, I think. She was a lot quieter though. Not moving much at all."

"That's probably good, right?"

"I guess so. Dr. Aragones didn't say anything new."

"That's got to be good," Karen said and smiled. She hugged me and we held each other tight. Thank goodness for her positivity. I took it as a reminder to try and do the same.

I drove to work for the first time since the previous Wednesday, back in what felt like a different life. I was teaching at Dutch Neck Elementary School in Princeton Junction, New Jersey. It is an older building that many staff lovingly (and not so lovingly) referred to as "Duct Tape Elementary."

I went to the counter in the front office to sign in. Next to the attendance book I noticed there were three new, bright-yellow ledger pads filled with dates and names. The pads were labeled: FOOD SHOPPING FOR KRECH FAMILY, MEALS FOR KRECH FAMILY and BABYSITTING FOR KRECH FAMILY. All of November's dates and most of December's were filled in. Obviously, word had spread among the whole staff, and here was the Dutch Neck school family in action.

I walked into my classroom. Completely familiar but somehow different now. Everything was different now. I read through the notes the substitute had left. Buses began pulling up in front of the building and my first little second-grader poked her head in the door and literally ran over to my desk. Breathlessly, she asked, "Mr. Krech, is it true you had a dead baby?"

Ah, the wonderful, uncensored directness of young kids. It's one of the reasons I love teaching elementary school. "No, not at all. Don't worry. I'll tell you all about it when everyone's here."

So I began the school day by gathering my class together on the carpet for a small talk. Normally, I would not be sharing this part of my life with eight-year-olds, but word was already out there somehow, so I had to deal with it.

"I missed you guys. I'm glad to be back," I started.

"What about your baby?" one of my boys asked.

"That's what I'm going to tell you about." Every eye was on me. I had to choose my words carefully. "Mrs. Krech had a baby girl, and the baby is very small. She needs special care, so she is going to stay in the hospital for a while."

"Is she sick?"

"Not really. She's small and needs extra care."

"So, she's not dead."

"No, she's okay."

"Are you still going to teach us?"

"Yes, of course. Who else are they going to get to teach you crazies?"

That made them laugh and we moved on to our plans for the day. As I saw my colleagues in the halls and at lunch, I gave them the adult version of the same talk. I wrote a letter to my class parents as well. I saw Melanie Faulkner in the hall. "Hey, Melanie.

I wanted you and Greg to know those verses are really helpful. I appreciate you guys doing that."

"Oh, no problem. And we'll be seeing you tonight. We're bringing over groceries. Can you give me a list sometime today?"

"Absolutely. Thank you so much." We shared a quick hug and both quickstepped back to our classrooms.

The rest of the day I was almost totally absorbed in my class (easy to do with a room full of eight-year-olds), except when I would glance at the school clock above the door. Every hour that would go by without a call, I would say a silent prayer of thanks. No news was very good news.

An hour after I got home from school, Melanie and Greg were at our front door, arms piled with brown grocery bags. Karen and Andrew were out taking a walk around the neighborhood.

Melanie and I were unloading the bags onto the kitchen table when she suddenly gasped, "Oh my gosh." She stood stock-still, staring at a package of butter in her hand.

She turned to look at me. Her eyes were wide. "Faith weighs the same as this butter."

Her simple comparison caught me off guard. I had already lost perspective on how shocking this actually was.

Karen and I planned go to the hospital together at about seven o'clock. for an evening hospital visit together at about seven o'clock. Andrew would stay at home with another teacher friend from school, Jan Grover. Jan was first in the babysitting rotation. Andrew already knew her from school get-togethers and loved seeing her. "Hi, Jan!" he greeted her when she arrived.

"Hi, Andrew. How are you?"

"Good. Can I watch *Beauty and the Beast?*" Andrew liked to get to the point.

"Of course," she said, then looked to us. "Can he?" she asked, laughing.

"No problem," I said. "I'll put it in."

This would probably be Andrew's five-hundredth viewing of *Beauty and the Beast.*

That night at the unit, the first thing I noticed about Faith were the three little yellow smiley faces on her chest. Her heart rate was monitored with electrodes attached to these small patches. The original ones had been plain white circles. Then they had been heart-shaped. Now we had happy faces. I loved these small, light touches like the monitor patches, the rocking chairs, and the bunny-rabbit border. Even though there was no ignoring the fact that we were in an intensive care unit for infants, it helped make everything a bit warmer.

Meera was on duty with Faith again. As we exchanged hellos, she backed up a few steps. "I'll give you some time alone with her," she said.

This made me smile. As if Karen and I were going to have a private conversation with Faith that the nurses shouldn't hear. Meera moved over to another baby while Karen and I leaned in over the warmer. Faith was awake and wriggling. It was actually reassuring to me to see that motion again. "Hey, Faith. How are you doing?" I asked.

"Hi, big girl," Karen said. She delicately stroked our baby's arm.

Faith squirmed and tensed in reply. Her alarm rang. A nurse strolled over, muted the alarm, watched the monitor for a few seconds, wrote on her clipboard, then walked away.

I cooed to Faith. She squirmed and kicked more. Maybe a minute passed and the alarm rang again. The same nurse returned and adjusted the oxygen, but the alarm continued ringing.

Then Meera was back. Both nurses stood there, arms crossed, eyes on the monitor. Karen and I moved over. We found each other's hands.

Another nurse joined us from across the room. Meera reached in the tray and lifted Faith up off of her back and onto her side. The second nurse began talking quietly to her, saying, "Come on, Faith, let's breathe."

The alarm blared on.

CHAPTER 17

A's and B's

Meera lifted Faith up off the tray again and gently placed her back down on her other side. In a voice barely above a whisper she asked the nurse at the respirator, "Can you come up on the oxygen just a bit more? Thank you."

The alarm did not pause. "Please mute that," Meera added.

There was silence. Karen's grip on my hand tightened. We pulled closer together. Faith was kicking her legs jerkily. The mute on the alarm only held for maybe a minute, then it screamed again. The nurses did not react, just stood still and watched.

Then a pause. It had stopped. It was over. Thank goodness.

Blaaaaaare. Oh my God, why wasn't she breathing?

The alarm stopped. The nurses remained fixed in their positions. One, two, three, four, five silent moments. A brief alarm again. And then a break. It was slowing.

It continued to ring intermittently maybe three more times until finally there was a blessed continuous silence. The only sound was the rhythmic thump of the respirator.

The two nurses who had assisted moved off without a word. Meera glanced back at us, then turned and wagged a finger at Faith as she scolded her theatrically, "Don't you go showing off in front of your parents like that, little girl!"

Karen and I stood there stunned, not knowing what to say. Meera shook her head and said reassuringly, "They all do this, you know. It's an apnea episode. It is very common."

I had read about apnea in the preemie literature. It's when breathing just stops. A premature baby's brain is so immature that there is not always an awareness that breathing should continue at all times. During sleep or sometimes when stressed, the babies simply stop breathing.

Bradychardia is similar to apnea, except instead of the cessation of breathing, the heart stops beating or beats very slowly. It often follows apnea. Breathing stops. Then the heart stops. I was pretty sure we had just seen both.

Meera explained, "If a baby has an episode like this, we try to bring them out of it by stimulating them with touch or talk or more oxygen. Sometimes just changing their position will help. We call these 'A's and B's.' Apnea and bradychardia."

I hoped we would not witness any more A's or B's up close and personal.

•••

On Friday, the thirteenth, I drove to the hospital for my 6:30 a.m. visit. As I entered from the scrub room, I saw Dr. Aragones. I joined her and we walked over to Faith's warmer together. I asked the inevitable, "How's Faith?"

Dr. Aragones lowered her mask and replied quietly, "Well, she is stable."

Coming from Dr. Aragones, I took that as a ringing endorsement. "That's really good to hear. Thank you," I said. I watched

Faith wriggling and struggling. We stood there silently until Dr. Aragones excused herself and moved off. No mention of potassium levels or anything else. Her lack of sharing made me a bit uneasy though.

Suzie then appeared at my side. "Guess what?" she bubbled. "We've been able to begin lowering Faith's rate a bit, and she's tolerating it. For the first time, she's starting to assist with her breathing."

"Really?" I wondered why Dr. Aragones had not mentioned this.

"Yes. This is a *huge* step. The machine is no longer supplying all of her breaths. If Faith shows any resistance or weakness, though, we'll adjust back to where she shows us that she's comfortable and can tolerate it."

Me, being Mr. Glass Half-Empty, I had to share my latest worry. "Last night when we were here, she stopped breathing completely."

Suzie waved a hand at me and scoffed, "Oh, they all do that." She said it like they all pee in their pants too.

I was very thankful the nurses felt comfortable sharing with us. Maybe the doctors just didn't want to get our hopes up. I looked at Faith and sent her a mental message. *Keep it going, Faith Catherine. Keep hanging in.*

I drove home and told Karen the good news about Faith starting to breathe on her own. "That's so great! I'll go this afternoon," she said. "I'll bring Andrew to your mother."

I went to school and prepared for my day. I had an almost

constant adrenaline flow. Faith was still alive and so I was grateful and energized. And now she was starting to breathe on her own!

"How's your baby?" one of my girls greeted me as the buses arrived. I was glad to be able to tell her, "She's doing very well." Student after student asked the same question, so along with our usual morning class meeting with calendar, weather, and the day's schedule, I began to include a quick baby report.

I was anxious to get home from school and hear how Karen's visit was. She greeted me at the door with an immediate summary: "All the same. She's doing okay."

We'd made it another day.

During our visit that night, when I got over to the warmer, I was jolted back by two big, blue, saucer-like eyes staring back at me. "Karen. Both eyes are open," I said, stunned.

"Oh my gosh, yeah," she said, smiling.

Faith's eyes were startlingly clear and so blue. I could see why nurses had been calling her beautiful. Her nose was tiny and delicate. She had thin, light blonde eyebrows that arched almost questioningly. And those blue, blue eyes. She was beautiful.

Meera strolled over, smiling. "You see her eyes? She wanted to see who her mother and father were."

Karen and I laughed out loud. Meera laughed too. We all three stood staring for a minute, then Meera urged, "You know, you should talk to her more. She can hear you and understand you. She recognizes your voices from in the womb. You watch her oxygen levels when you talk. You will see them go up."

I just mumbled, "Sure, okay" and nodded. But that was not

near good enough for Meera. "Go ahead now," she insisted.

Karen and I bent dutifully over and began talking. "Hey, little girl. Hello, cutie. Hi, Faith." We repeated the typical baby babble every parent uses. We talked for about three or four minutes.

"Look. Look." Meera pointed to the oxygen saturation display—it had moved from ninety-five to ninety-eight. It was amazing. It really worked. As Karen put it afterward, "It's one more thing we can do to help."

Meera was obviously pleased with our reactions. "You can make cassette tapes of the two of you talking or singing or reading stories," she instructed. "They like that. We can play the tapes when you are not here. That way she can always hear you."

This all sounded a bit embarrassing, but who was going to refuse Meera? Besides, if it was good for Faith, I was all for it.

•••

First thing Saturday morning, I was at Radio Shack buying a mini tape recorder and a pack of tiny cassettes. It looked like something for James Bond, but it had to fit easily in Faith's little warmer tray. Karen and I sat down and taped ourselves taking turns reading *Goodnight Moon* and then doing some talking to Faith. It was about an hour's worth of listening.

We visited the NICU together later that morning and found Meera on duty again. I noticed the same nurses—Meera, Pam, Beth, Suzie, and a few others—were being repeatedly assigned to Faith. I guessed that they were the veterans and were up for dealing with someone that critical.

As we entered from the scrub room, I spotted another of

Faith's regular nurses, Kate, at the nurses' station in street clothes: a fashionable leather jacket, dark pants, and white sweater. She was distinctive looking, with long blonde hair and a big smile. This was the first time I'd seen a NICU nurse in regular clothes.

We exchanged greetings with Meera and showed her our newly purchased mini tape recorder and our first homemade tape. "That's very good," she said approvingly. "We can keep it right here. I will let the other nurses know to play it." She put it on the bottom rack of the warmer tray.

With the tapes, the talking, and the touching, it was becoming more and more clear that the care in the Mercer NICU was not just medicine and monitors.

I looked at Faith. She appeared more settled. There was less of the straining and tensing that we'd seen before.

"Did you see Kate this morning?" Meera asked, smiling.

Karen answered, "Yes, but we didn't get to talk to her."

Meera lowered her voice. "You know, she is here on her day off. She stopped in just to see how Faith is doing."

"I had no idea. That is so nice." It was quite a surprise. I was feeling very encouraged by this wonderful group of nurses.

Meera leaned in to us. "She told me she has a picture of Faith at home on her refrigerator. In fact, several of us do."

"That's so great," Karen said.

I bent over to check Faith's chart. Next to WEIGHT it was clearly marked—420 grams.

Faith was sinking further under a pound.

CHAPTER 18

Thy Will

I turned to Meera. Trying to keep any anxiety out of my voice, I asked, "Faith is down to four hundred twenty grams?" It was a question, but probably came out sounding like an accusation.

Meera shook her head dismissively. "That's nothing. That's expected." She gestured at the respirator. "Just look at her oxygen needs. She's getting only thirty percent oxygen now, and her rate is only thirty. She is doing much, much more of the breathing on her own. She is doing very, very good."

Thirty percent was way better than the 90 percent Faith had needed just days ago, and she did look more settled too.

When we got home later that morning, my mother, the babysitter, greeted us. "Hi," she said with a wink. "I don't know what happened to Andrew. He was just here. But now he's gone. He must have run away."

"Oh no," Karen replied. "That's terrible."

"Well, we'll just have to buy a dog instead," I joked.

Andrew leaped out from behind the family room couch, seizing my leg and yelling, "Got ya!"

I bent down quickly and lifted him up by the ankles. "Oh yeah?" I said. I wrestled him onto the carpet and let him reverse me onto my back. I lay there pinned and helpless with a triumphant two-year-old kneeling on my chest. It felt great. I was more thankful than ever that we had a child. I tried to imagine Faith as a two-year-old, playing and wrestling around here in the family room with us.

I couldn't do it.

Later that afternoon, I knelt by my bed. I was praying almost constantly in my head throughout the day, but sometimes I just felt drawn to stop, kneel, and pray. I prayed, *Please, God. Let Faith have a future playing together with Andrew and me here someday.*

I wondered what she would look like if she did. Would she be terribly thin and weak like now? Would she be in a wheelchair? Stop, I chided myself. How about some belief? *Oh God,* I prayed, *have patience with me, please.* I read my two verses again: *"Ask and ye shall receive." "Have faith as small as a mustard seed and move mountains."*

We spent the rest of that Saturday grocery shopping, visiting my family, and playing with Andrew. It was clear my mother and father were hesitant to ask how the baby was. I kept giving them brief summaries, but I didn't much mention the negatives. Only my father had actually seen Faith.

That night, even though our evening visit was uneventful, I woke up at 1:00 a.m. and couldn't get back to sleep. I did some tossing and turning and pillow moving. Two o'clock came and I was still awake. My thoughts turned to Faith. Dr. Hecht had mentioned that the NICU had a twenty-four-hour visitation policy for parents. I decided to try it out.

It was freezing cold in the middle of the night in mid-November

New Jersey. The sky was black, clear, and speckled brightly with stars. I had the dark, icy streets of Trenton all to myself and my little car. I parked in the almost-empty hospital lot and waved to the security guard on my way in. I recognized all the guards now, and they knew who I was since I was probably there as often as some of them.

In contrast to the cold, inhospitable night, the NICU was warm and welcoming. I took my time scrubbing up with the nice hot water, then went directly to Faith's warmer. There was my girl, wires and tubes everywhere, but still and quiet. Peg appeared next to me. "She's doing fine," she offered quietly. No questioning me about why I was there at two in the morning. Just acceptance.

It was comforting to see Peg physically watching over Faith while Karen and I were home asleep. I thought about Kate coming in on her day off and the other nurses with pictures of Faith on their refrigerators. I felt a peace with our baby being looked after by these kind, caring professionals. Maybe that's why I came. To just see and feel that.

Or maybe it had something to do with my drive home.

I was stopped at a red light when I turned on the radio and started scanning through the dial. As I did, I came across a station that, it quickly became clear, was Christian programming. Usually I dialed right through any "religious" stations and concurred with Andrew's comments when he'd heard his first radio preacher: "I don't like that man yelling." It always seemed like it was either a guy yelling at you to repent or old, slow, off-key, organ-drenched hymns.

This was different though. "That man" on the radio at 3:00 a.m. turned out to be Steve Brown. His show was called *Key Life*. He was interesting, and he wasn't yelling. It's funny, but I can't remember exactly what he talked about. The message and the tone hit me the right way though. I listened all the way home and flopped into bed feeling content.

The next morning, Sunday, the fifteenth, I slept late and awoke to the smell of pancakes. In the kitchen, Andrew and Karen were already eating. I said, "I'm going to go in and see Faith and then be back for eleven o'clock Mass. If you can, save me a couple of those, please."

"Of course," Karen said.

"Mmmm! Maybe," Andrew replied. A remark that earned him a severe tickling.

I was very curious about the station I had heard the night before and turned on the radio as soon as I got in the car. After a commercial, an announcer came on. "This is WCHR, 94.5 FM, in Trenton, New Jersey. And now *The Alternative* with Pastor Tony Evans. Today Dr. Evans will be focusing on the Lord's Prayer."

After only a few minutes of driving and listening it became clear that the gist of this talk focused on just one phrase from the Lord's Prayer, "Thy will be done." Dr. Evans spoke plainly and emphatically. "We as Christians are to pray that *God's* will be done. This is how Jesus instructed us to pray when He was asked. Now take notice. The prayer does not say *my* will, but *thy* will," he pointed out. "Remember. This is how Jesus taught us to pray. Not *your* will, not *my* will, not your Grandma's will, but *His* will.

"And—*and*—His will might not agree with your will. It might not even seem like it makes any sense at all. But— You've got to come to accept that someone who knows a lot better than you about what should happen is in control. You must learn to accept God's will, whatever it might be."

Before I knew it, I was in front of the hospital. I pulled over to the curb and sat there. I didn't want to get out of the car. National Public Radio calls it a "driveway moment." The program is so engaging, you don't want to shut the car off and get out, so you sit in your driveway listening.

I had been praying the Lord's Prayer since I was six years old, but most of the time I was chanting it along with a couple of hundred other people in church, like the Pledge of Allegiance. It occurred to me at that moment, there in the street, that I had never thought about reciting a prayer as *speaking* to God. And with good reason. Because reciting something is not speaking to someone.

I guess some of this came from when we were kids and went to confession. The priest would hear our sins and then assign us penance, usually in the form of saying a certain number of Our Fathers or Hail Marys. It didn't feel so much like you were talking with God if you were rattling the words off ten times in a row. It was more like doing pushups.

Finally forcing myself to turn off the radio and get out of the car, I flew up the concrete steps to the hospital front door. I headed down the hall to the chapel and knelt in a pew.

It was my will that Faith live, but what was God's will? I knelt and prayed, *God, thank you for all you have done for Faith. I pray that it might be your will that Faith live. But if not—I resolve to accept that as best I can.*

And even if it is your will that Faith be with us for only a short time, I will try to appreciate and make the most of that time. Thank you for this time with her. Please help me to accept your will, and be thankful for whatever it may be. Amen.

The precariousness of Faith's existence made me think of that classic description of life as a "vapor" or a "mist." I had always found this notion more than a little frightening. I didn't even like to think about it.

I remembered back in college riding on a campus bus with another student I knew named Anne. Gary, the young air force evangelist on my dorm floor, had introduced me to her when he had tried to get me to join their Bible study. I guess he figured, very accurately, that if there were girls there, I might come.

It had been a particularly bright and sunny afternoon as we rode back together from a class on the main campus to our dorms. She looked out the window, staring up at a cerulean blue sky and puffy, white clouds. "It's so beautiful," she said. "I bet it will be like this when we meet Jesus." Then she looked from the window to me. "I can't wait to see Him," she added brightly.

My immediate thought was, whoa, that means you'll be dead! Fortunately, I had the presence of mind to just smile and nod.

There is a country song that features the refrain "Everybody wants to go to heaven, but nobody wants to go now." So true. For me, at least. I wasn't so sure about Anne.

But now, with Faith, it was different. I didn't suddenly have a death wish, but for the first time, there was some comfort in the idea that life on earth is short. If Faith were to die, there was hope that I would see her again in eternity with Jesus Christ. Life here on earth was short. Life in heaven was loooooong. Like eternal. I had heard all this before, of course. I knew about it in an academic sense. Just like you know the Grand Canyon is a big, deep hole. But until you are there and right up close to it standing on the edge, you really have no idea what BIG and DEEP is. Same turned out to be true with God. It was no longer academic. It was BIG and DEEP.

As I knelt there in the chapel, I came to the conclusion that accepting the possible brevity of Faith's life was not at odds with asking for the miracle that she be saved. I had originally thought that it was a big cop-out to pray for something and then if it didn't happen, you'd fall back on "Well, it was God's will." So much for faith in prayer, right?

But pushed along by Dr. Evans's words, I consciously turned it all over to God that morning. He was in control. He would know best. We had asked for a miracle; God could do them as promised, but only if it was going to be best for us.

I ended my prayers with *Let your will be done*. And perhaps for the first time ever, I meant it, as much as I humanly could.

CHAPTER 19

Dr. Syed

From the chapel, I climbed the back stairs up to the NICU and headed straight for Faith's warmer. I zeroed in on her chart. 440 grams. Still under a pound, but a gain was a gain.

I smoothed the little patch of blonde fluff on her head. "Hey, big girl," I said softly. She stretched her arms and legs out. A very normal baby motion. That was reassuring too.

Pam strolled over. "Hey, I'm going to give Faith a bath. You want to watch?"

"Sure." I wondered how you gave a baby like this a bath. Then she mentioned that Dr. Aragones was on duty. This made me uneasy. Unfortunately, it looked like Dr. Aragones was going to be there most of the day, almost every day.

Pam was always so straightforward; I knew I could ask her. "Is Dr. Aragones in charge here?"

As she answered, Pam began "bathing" Faith with a bit of gauze and warm water. "Yes," she said. "She's acting director."

Pam worked the gauze under Faith's arms and down her sides. "Since the NICU started here at Mercer, we had one director. He was head neonatologist for eight years. Then in October, just before Faith joined us, he resigned kind of suddenly. We still had part-time neonatologists like Dr. Hecht, and they took on more hours, but there was no full-time director."

Pam dried Faith with another piece of gauze. "Dr. Aragones is acting director now, but she's only been here a few weeks. She's alternating two-to-four-week shifts with another neonatologist from Florida, Dr. Bernard."

I had hoped to hear something that would boost my confidence in Dr. Aragones, like how she had been there for years. Not a few weeks.

•••

Later that morning, Karen, Andrew, and I went to church. To be honest, most of the time in the past I went to church more out of a sense of duty than anything else. I had been taught that God wanted me there, and on some childish level I felt like if I put in my hours, I would be okay with God. Now my attitude was different and so was my participation. I wanted to be there to learn and pray. I was praying as if it were life and death. Because it was.

During Mass I used to hope the readings and the homily would be short so that we could get out early and get on with what we needed to do. Now I wanted to hear more. I left Mass pumped up.

As we drove home, Karen said, "I'm planning on tutoring Raymond again. And I should get back to writing for ETS."

Karen had been tutoring a young boy for several years, as well as doing freelance writing for Educational Testing Service's ESL exams. "Sure," I replied. "There's no reason not to."

It felt weird to keep doing normal things like working, because it was all colored by this abnormal state where the big overriding thing each day was Faith.

That night we returned to the hospital just after 5:30 p.m. Faith had made it a full week. Now 5:30 p.m. was my marker for when a day ended and a new one started, since that was the time she'd been born. It was like FST, Faith Standard Time.

Meera greeted us as we made our way over. "I have some news," she said. She leaned toward us, obviously excited. "Dr. Syed is on duty tonight. He is going to move Faith's breathing tube from her mouth to her nose. It is better for her that way." She nodded at us as she spoke, which made me nod back in agreement. "He has to thread the tube through one of her nostrils, down her windpipe, and into her lungs, but he is very good. You will get to meet him."

Syed sounded Middle Eastern to me. "Where is he from?" I asked.

Meera said, "He is Egyptian."

A Middle East connection, I thought. That would give us some common ground.

Dr. Syed ambled in a little while later. He was a bit portly and moved in a leisurely, relaxed manner. He was accompanied by a nurse and they went directly over to Faith. Karen and I were off to the side, with Meera. She said, "Dr. Syed usually works a couple of the nights during the week, and once or twice a month he takes the weekend shift, from Friday night through Monday morning."

Karen and I stayed where we were, but we could still see most of what was going on. A 1-pound baby's nostril is not a big target. It was a very thin tube, but it was a miniscule nostril. It was surprising and impressive to me how this large man, with fingers that resembled sausages, worked so delicately on so tiny an infant.

One of the nurses remarked later, "We didn't think he could do it, but he did."

Dr. Syed disappeared after the procedure, returning half an hour later with a huge Styrofoam cup of steaming coffee in one hand, reaching out his other to shake ours. I greeted him by saying, "As-salaam-alaikum," a bit of Arabic I had learned while in Saudi.

He smiled broadly in surprise. "Alaikum-as-salaam," he replied. "And where did you learn Arabic?"

I told him about our time in Saudi. We started talking about life in the Middle East. He was listening and chatting, leaning his considerable bulk on the respirator with his elbow, white-sneakered feet casually crossed in front of him on the linoleum floor. I steered the conversation to my inevitable "So, how's she doing?"

"How is she doing? She's doing GREAT!" he boomed. He said "GREAT!" like Tony the Tiger from the Frosted Flakes commercials, if Tony the Tiger had been Egyptian.

"How old is she?" he asked. "Eight days? When is her due date?"

"March sixth," Karen said.

"In March, she will be walking out of here," he exclaimed.

We laughed out loud at his audacity.

He continued with enthusiasm, "We are working with QUALITY here. You can see that. Look how well she is doing! Plus, it is good she is a girl. Boys do not do as well as girls in this situation. Statistically, black girls do the best, then white girls, then black boys, then white boys." He smiled and shrugged. "Too bad she is not a black girl, but with you two, that would be difficult."

It felt light years better than being told again that Faith was critical but stable. More importantly, it was clear that Dr. Syed believed what he was saying. He wasn't just painting a rosy picture for our benefit. Faith was special. She was "quality." And something was definitely going on in her favor. We thanked him and practically floated home. A week old and "doing GREAT!"

CHAPTER 20

Prayer Sessions

I woke up early, excited to get over to the hospital. It was Monday, November 16. Day 9 on the "Faith Calendar." Dr. Syed's enthusiasm was contagious. Faith was doing great!

She did look good too. Just more settled with less straining and contortions. I checked her chart. 440 grams. I deflated a little. Weight was a fact. Not an opinion. Faith had yet to gain even a single gram. A gram is like a piece of popcorn and I knew weight was important for her health and strength.

I spotted Dr. Aragones in her light blue scrubs, still with the white surgical mask pulled up tight. She noticed me and made her way over. After exchanging hellos, I asked how Faith was doing and she replied once again, "She is critical but stable."

I had come to appreciate that "stable" was a very, very good thing. "That's great to hear. Thank you," I responded. "But is her weight a problem? She doesn't seem to be gaining at all."

She nodded slightly. "Yes. We are trying to get her weight up and supply her with all the nutrition she needs, but we cannot accomplish this entirely by the IV." She sat down on a stool. "I am thinking she is ready to begin gavage feeding. This is where we run a tube down the throat and into the belly. There is a cap at the top, which attaches to a syringe. The food is administered slowly over

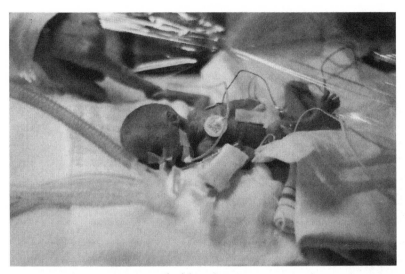

One month old in the warmer tray

Karen with Faith at two months

Two years old at the Museum of Science in Boston

Faith loving birds in 2019

time through the tube directly into the stomach by gravity and air pressure."

This was the most detail Dr. Aragones had ever shared with me about anything and I wanted to keep it going. "So she would get more food this way?" I asked.

"Yes. It should help. But there are risks. We have to be careful and move slowly so we don't overburden her system. We want to avoid NEC."

She pronounced it "neck." The full term was necrotizing enterocolitis. I had read about it. Premature infants badly need nourishment so they can put on weight, gain strength, and fight infections. However, their digestive systems, particularly the bowels, are not ready to handle food except via the placenta, which is long gone.

NEC is caused by food that is not properly digested or excreted, and instead begins to sit and putrefy in the bowels. This leads to infection, then bleeding, and ultimately destruction of the tissue. Many preemies with NEC require surgery to remove sections of intestine. Some die from it.

It was another balancing act. Too much food and NEC could result. Too little and the baby doesn't gain weight or strength and is more susceptible to infection or doesn't have the strength to fight one off once contracted.

"Yes. I think we may try soon," she concluded.

"Thank you for letting me know," I said. I wondered if maybe before, Dr. Aragones was not sharing much because it was all bad news. Anything anyone in the NICU said or did, I found myself weighing for every possible nuance.

Sure enough, we got to see gavage feeding up close that evening. Faith's first feed was administered by one of her regular nurses, Red-Haired Debbie. There was also Dark-Haired Debbie. They were both tall, large women with the same first and last names. Karen and I started using the hair-color designation to keep them straight.

Red-Haired Debbie was cheery, redheaded, and freckled. Her hands were pretty large, which made the syringe look even tinier than it might have. She held it up so gravity could do its work. "Here you go, Faith. This stuff is yucky, but it's all we can give you right now," she confided.

I looked at the gray sludge in the syringe. "What is that?" I asked.

Debbie grinned. "Predigested formula. Pretty appetizing, huh? I'll put some aside for you." She winked as she pushed the plunger. The sludge nudged slowly down the tube. She passed it over to Karen. "Here. Do you want to feed her, Mom?" she asked.

I had to smile. This was feeding a baby? Karen held the tube up and we watched the liquid disappear. Later, Debbie inserted the yellow plunger and reversed the suction to see if all the food had been absorbed.

"Good girl, Faith. Way to eat it all up," Debbie commented. She turned to Karen. "If there was any residual, we'd measure it and record it. If she's leaving a lot, we'll cut back on the amount to avoid any chance of NEC."

I was hopeful that maybe this was the key to Faith finally

gaining some weight.

The next morning, Tuesday, I went in before school and immediately checked the chart to see what kind of weight gain the gavage feeding had produced. 440 grams. I checked the date. November 17. No weight gain. Faith was moving and kicking up a storm. I looked at the nurse, who shrugged. "Active girl."

I told Karen about it at breakfast.

"Well, at least she's not losing," she replied. Karen's simple statement again reminded me to look at the positive side.

"That's true," I admitted.

Then Karen told me, "Suzanne called while you were at the hospital. She asked if she could come along to visit with me this afternoon."

Suzanne was a close family friend we had known for years. "What did you tell her?" I asked. My youngest sister, Dorothy, was flying in to see us, and I was sure she would ask to see Faith too.

"I said I thought it would be all right. It would be hard to tell her no."

I kind of wondered how that would go, but I said, "Okay with me."

That afternoon, Karen brought Faith her first visitor other than my dad. When Suzanne saw Faith, her hand flew to her mouth. "Oh my God," she gasped. Tears followed. She was literally shaking.

Though the visit eventually went well, it reminded us again that even though Karen and I had grown somewhat used to Faith's appearance, it was literally shocking to anyone outside the NICU.

•••

Faith's second week of life proceeded into Wednesday, the eighteenth. I went into the chapel that morning and prayed the Lord's Prayer, aiming to squeeze meaning out of every word. I emphasized the "us" in the line "Give us this day our daily bread." "Us" included Faith, of course. I ended with, *Thank you for another day with Faith. God, I will do my best to accept your will.*

After our evening visit, I got home, went up to our bedroom, and pulled out our little Bible. Even though I'd been told by the nuns since I was five years old that that was the Word of God, it was finally hitting home in a very real way. Certainly, if God personally wrote me a letter, I would read it with extreme attention, so I probably should read and think seriously about what He'd already said.

I found and reread my two special passages a couple of times, but since they were both in Matthew, I figured I'd start reading the entire Gospel of Matthew from the beginning, a chapter each day. It was actually an exciting notion. If you had told me a month before that I would be excited about reading the Bible, I would have told you that you definitely had the wrong guy.

The next morning I got in the car and turned on the radio. It was still set on WCHR. I had found another local Christian radio station as well, WAWZ, also known as Star 99.1.

Tony Evans was on again. I will never forget his sermon that morning. I'm still praying from this today.

Dr. Evans was talking about Mark, chapter 9, verses 14 through 27. He said, "In this story, a father brings his son to Jesus. The son has been plagued since childhood with seizures that have the young man convulsing, falling on the ground, foaming at the mouth, jumping in the fire. The poor father pleads with Jesus, 'If you can do anything, have compassion on us and help us.'

"So what does Jesus do? He tells them, 'If you can believe, all things are possible to him who believes.' Did you hear that? ALL things are possible IF you can believe. It's the old IF-THEN."

In the story, the father immediately cries out and says with tears, "Lord, I believe; help my unbelief."

Dr. Evans asked, "Is this you? Is this how you pray? Do you pray unbelieving God will answer?"

Yes! *That was exactly me.* I believed, but I was still constantly worried, so what kind of belief was that? I needed help with it, so I prayed about it. *Lord, I believe; help my unbelief.* I started praying it right then and there. The Bible knew what was what.

Trying to read these scriptures in my flimsy little Bible with the tiny print made me want to get one that was easier to get into, with bigger pages and bigger print. I wasn't sure if regular bookstores had Bibles so I checked the phone book hoping I might find a Christian bookstore. I found eight. In fact, there was one right in the next town, Princeton. Who knew? On Wednesday after work, I drove to Lamplighter Books.

The store turned out to be a neatly painted, two-story Victorian row house on Nassau Street, the main drag in Princeton. I parked behind the building and sat there. It was ridiculous, but I was apprehensive about the people who worked in the store. I worried that they might be like those evangelists on the street who come up to you and try to get you to answer questions like "If you died today, where would you go?" Would they swoop down on me and ask me if I was saved and then make me prove it somehow? I didn't know what I would say.

Finally I sucked it up, got out of the car, and headed for the back entrance. I decided whatever they tried, I could handle it. If they started asking me a lot of hard questions, I could always pretend that I didn't understand English. I could switch to Arabic and shrug a lot.

I opened the door and was greeted by soft classical music. Brightly lit white shelves lined with Christian books, CDs, videos, and magazines filled the room. A few people were shopping. The woman at the register nodded and said hello. No one swooped.

I wandered around amazed at all this stuff. I had never seen anything like it before. I made my way into another room that was packed with Bibles on all four walls. There must have been at least fifty different ones. Almost immediately I found one I really liked, *The Word in Life Study Bible* (New King James Version). It was easy to read and understand and full of sidebar historical notes, explanations, and commentary. And the print was big. I also grabbed a devotional called *Time with God: The New Testament for Busy People*. There were about six or seven other things I wanted to buy. I had never seen anything like this before.

I had been in the middle of reading John Grisham's *The Firm* when Faith was born. It was an absorbing read and I had been enjoying it, but my interest in it had vanished completely. Compared to the Word of God, in my present circumstances, Grisham's fictional tale was pretty insignificant stuff.

The next afternoon, Karen brought my sister Dorothy in to visit. She reported that it went better than with Suzanne, but it was clear that Dorothy was unnerved as well. In the evening, Karen and I beelined into the NICU and checked the chart together— still 440 grams. "She's not gaining at all," I said.

Karen shared a small, hopeful smile. "She seems to be doing okay, though, right? I mean her breathing and everything is so much better."

I had to admit, yes.

Dr. Syed was on duty, so after some brief small talk, I shared my latest concern with him. "What do you think about Faith not gaining weight?"

He smiled and patted his ample stomach. "What? Do you want her to look like me?" he joked.

"Well, maybe a little slimmer," I replied. "And no mustache."

He laughed, then said, "We have been continuing the gavage feedings very conservatively, with tiny increments of breast milk being added to the formula each day. We don't want NEC, right?"

I nodded agreement. We definitely did not want NEC.

He nodded toward Karen. "And fortunately, your wife has provided us with plenty of breast milk. So that's very helpful."

"Right. I know. That is good" is what I said. But I was thinking how they were doing all of this and Faith was still not gaining at all. She would be susceptible to infection. She wouldn't have the strength to breathe. She wouldn't be able to handle food.

Dr. Syed could sense my fear, I'm sure. He put a big, meaty hand on my shoulder. He gave me a wry smile. "You have to be patient, my friend. She will get there. Believe me, someday soon she will be beating you up."

I laughed out loud, but in my head I was already praying my new prayer. *Lord, I believe. Please help my unbelief.*

CHAPTER 21

A Public Faith

The tune he was singing was Stevie Wonder's "He's Misstra Know-It-All," and Daryle, the guard behind the security desk, was pointing right at me. "He's the man, with the plan. He's Mr. Faith's Daaaaaad." Other than "Happy Birthday," this was a first for me.

Daryle was a tall, thin, dapper guy with a wonderful voice. It was now the nineteenth of November. Day 11 for Faith. And I had a small mission in mind for this morning.

We shook hands and embraced. "How are you, sir?" he asked.

"I'm fine. Thanks. How are you?"

He pointed toward heaven. "Thank God, doing well. And your baby's good too." He nodded. "Yeah. Mmm-hmm. I just spoke to the nurses coming off duty."

"That's great to hear," I said. I loved getting this informal, behind-the-scenes scoop. We shook hands again. "Thanks for letting me know."

I went into the chapel and knelt and prayed. Then I got up and silently read my two verses from the large Bible on the altar. I deliberately left it open to Matthew 7, with the intention that someone else might see the verses and receive help from them just as I had.

In fact, I had both verses in my shirt pocket. I had written them neatly on three-by-five index cards with the intention of putting them up somewhere near Faith. That was my little mission. I don't know why I wanted to do this, but sometimes you just have to go with your intuition. Or the prodding of the Holy Spirit.

In the NICU, I found Faith in her tray, sleeping on her back, one arm above her head, the other at her side. A peaceful baby girl in a classic restful pose. A glance at her chart showed her weight. 440 grams. Still.

Dark-Haired Debbie was on duty.

"Hi, Debbie. How's she doing?"

"She's stable." She paused a second, then added, "She's doing well."

"That's great," I replied. I don't think Debbie was completely at ease with me yet, but I had the index cards with me and so I held them up and asked her, "Would it be okay if I taped these two cards on the warmer?" I felt a little uncomfortable, but also compelled at the same time. Full disclosure: "They have a couple of Bible verses on them."

Debbie didn't hesitate. "Sure. I'll get you some tape."

In situations where people were sick, injured, or in the hospital, most Catholics I knew would put up a cross or a medal. This seemed kind of mystical or maybe just more symbolic. Nobody I knew put up verses. It was too specific or blatant or something. But I felt pulled to publicly acknowledge, in a small way, that I believed that prayer was at work with this little girl and that these verses were important.

Debbie brought the tape and watched as I put the cards up on the side of the warmer. "Thanks," I said as I finished.

"No problem," she replied. She paused. "I've seen those before somewhere. I like them. They're very nice," she added awkwardly. We shared a smile, then I headed off to school.

School was as busy as ever and was actually a huge help in keeping my mind diverted. We began the day with reading, then moved into writing, where my second graders were creating their own stories about everything from dinosaurs to birthday parties to space to dinosaurs having birthday parties in space.

At the end of the day, I started my drive home, but then stopped at a church about a quarter mile from the school. I felt like praying. I knew I didn't have to be physically in a church to pray, but it just felt right.

When I got to the front doors, I found they were locked. I stood there for a second. I could get back in the car and pray in there or just come back tomorrow. But I felt the same impulse again. I wanted to show God and anyone around me that prayer was important and I was not ashamed or embarrassed by my belief, but that I was beginning to own it.

I knelt down in front of the church doors, the concrete sidewalk digging into my knees, and prayed my thanks.

Prayer was definitely on my mind when I got home. Karen greeted me at the door with a hug and kiss. "How's your day?" she asked brightly.

I was thankful that Karen continued to maintain this warm positivity. I hung up my coat. "It went well. How's Faith?"

"I was there about two o'clock. She's doing fine."

"How's her rate?"

"I think it's about the same."

I paused. I tried not to ask, but could not help myself. "Did you write it down?"

As soon as the words left my mouth, I regretted it.

"No. It was *about the same*," she added pointedly.

I took a breath and a step back. Karen and I are very different people in a number of ways. I am a planner. Karen is spontaneous. I get up early. She sleeps late. I like to stay home. She likes to go out. Our approach to interacting with the NICU staff was one more example of our differences.

We sat down together on the family room couch. I wanted to change the subject and I was wondering if Karen was feeling the same pull to prayer that I was, so it was a good time to ask. "Kar, when you go into the hospital, in the afternoon, have you been stopping in the chapel?"

Karen nodded. "Every time."

"Yeah. Me too."

"It's just so private and quiet," she said. We snuggled closer as she wiped a tear away. "It's like when I go in there, all my emotions just flow. I can pray and put all the emotion into words."

"What do you pray?" I asked.

Karen smiled. "Mostly, 'God, please keep her strong. Let her gain weight. Let her be healthy.'"

Andrew scooted into the room. He climbed up on the couch and squirmed in between us. "Why are you guys whispering?" he whispered.

I whispered back, "We're not whispering. We're talking."

"About me?" he said with a grin.

"Yeah," I said. "That you're a goose." I began tickling him and he rolled off onto the floor laughing.

"Yeah. I know what you mean about the chapel," I said to Karen.

Andrew sang, "Blah, blah, blah" and pulled on my leg. I tumbled onto the floor and let him conquer me once again.

Karen smiled. "When I'm up in the NICU, I try to keep my emotions in check. I just talk about information and facts. Even though the nurses are always upbeat and positive, I don't want to let my feelings go there. I can in the chapel. With God."

"Yep," I grunted through the sharp little knees on my chest. "Me too."

Karen and I had been married twelve years, had two children, been through three miscarriages, and lived on three continents together, but we were just now having our first real conversation about prayer.

•••

My mom and dad stopped by to watch Andrew that night. As I took her coat, my mom hesitated and then whispered, "How is everything?"

"She's holding steady," I answered. "They say she's a real fighter."

She nodded and smiled. Wiping away a tear, she said, "Good. I'm still praying for her."

I hugged her. "I know. Thanks, Mom. Keep doing that, please."

My dad was already being led by Andrew to the basement, where most of the toys were. Karen's mom lived about an hour away and didn't drive, so most of what she knew about Faith was what Karen shared over the phone. Still, we knew Faith was in everyone's prayers.

When Karen and I got to the unit, we found Faith looking quiet and calm, but still so thin. Then, as if emerging from sleep, she stretched and writhed. She was twitching like she was having a seizure. Was she? My worries were interrupted by a loud "Hi!"

I looked up into a round, smiling, pink face. It was Kim. Karen's nurse from the delivery. "How are you guys doing?" she asked cheerily.

Karen and I exchanged hugs with her. "Oh my gosh," Karen exclaimed. "How are you?"

We hadn't seen Kim since that first night. I looked back at Faith. She had resettled and was calm again.

"I'm fine," Kim answered. "How's it going with you two?"

Karen said, "We're okay. Just trying to keep things moving in a positive direction."

"Day eleven," I remarked.

Kim looked down into the warmer. "She's doing really well, you know."

Karen grinned. "Really?"

She answered enthusiastically, "Oh yeah. She's really hanging in there."

When a nurse said something like this, that she was a fighter, that she was hanging in, it made me feel great, but it also made me wonder what it was like for Faith. Most likely a struggle for each breath. Straining to make underdeveloped lungs do a job they weren't ready to do.

"I brought her something," Kim said. She reached in the pocket of her scrubs and took out a small, white jewelry box. She handed it to Karen. "This was mine. I got it on my first communion, but I'd like to give it to her."

Karen opened the box. Sitting on a bed of cotton was a silver-and-white communion medal. "Oh, it's beautiful. Are you sure?"

Kim replied ardently, "Yes. I want her to have it."

Karen hugged Kim again. "Thank you so much." She sighed. "It's lovely." Karen pinned the medal onto one of the Bible verse cards. Now we had the Catholic side of things covered.

Through that week and into the next, it was essentially the same report each day. Faith's oxygen usage was inching down. She was doing a pretty good job taking in her food with the gavage, but unfortunately her weight remained stubbornly around 440 grams, a gram or two up one day, a few down the next. No real improvement.

Things were mainly positive and if not moving forward as rapidly as I hoped, at least she was stable. On Wednesday, November 25, the night before Thanksgiving, she was seventeen days old.

Karen and I walked over to her tray that evening to find Pam with Faith. We greeted her with our usual "How's she doing?"

Pam looked up and said, "Well, she has an infection."

CHAPTER 22

Infection

I tried hard not to freak out, but ended up stammering, "D-d-did she have a fever? Does she have a fever?"

Pam continued setting up an IV line. "No. She just wasn't acting like herself. She was too antsy. So we did some blood work and her white count was way up. We started her on these antibiotics, and she'll be on them for the next ten days."

Tim Hall had warned us this was going to happen, but I had hoped that in our case he would be wrong. He had also said, "If she gets through the infection, she should be okay." And if she didn't...

Faith didn't look any different than she had earlier in the week. But Pam had noticed. I also didn't get the sense that Pam was panicking, but then, she was always calm and steady.

In the scrub room on our way out, we were surprised to see Dr. Livney, one of Karen's ob-gyn group. He greeted us with an upbeat "Hi, how are you guys doing?" I was still absorbing the bad news, but forced a weak smile as we shook hands. "I saw your daughter," he said. "She's doing great."

I figured he hadn't heard yet, so thought I had better let him know the latest. "Well, yeah, but we just found out that she has an infection."

He smiled right through that bombshell. "Yes, I know, but it's bacterial and not viral, so it's a much less serious thing. And they caught it early. She's doing really, really well," he said enthusiastically. "Aside from infection, the thing to watch for now is NEC." He then began explaining about NEC.

I was half listening to that. I knew about NEC, but I was thinking instead about how here was a doctor, kind of on the outside of things, who knew the medical details of the situation with the infection, and he was not panicking or negative, so maybe I shouldn't be either.

Here we go again, I thought. *Oh Lord, I believe. Help me with my unbelief.*

•••

Thanksgiving Day started off with Andrew parading around the house in his paper-bag Native American vest and headband. He had made it with Karen, and he put it on as soon as he got out of bed.

We dropped him off at my parents' so he could show them his outfit and then we headed to the hospital. Meera met us there with a cheery "Happy Thanksgiving!"

The three of us walked over to the warmer together. Faith was asleep, curled on her side wrapped in a yellow blanket. I searched her for signs of the infection. Meera read my mind and jumped in right away to reassure me. "Look how peaceful. Everyone knows she is doing very good."

Despite Meera's cheery pronouncements, I had to ask. "How's she making out with the infection?"

I got another reproachful look for that one. "You can see she is doing very good," she said sternly.

I was embarrassed and quickly changed the subject. "I was surprised Dr. Livney knew about her. We saw him here yesterday."

"Oh yes. All of the doctors in that group have been checking on her."

"Really?"

"Yes. Dr. Baumann. Dr. Livney. Dr. Druker. They all come."

I had no idea they had been doing this. It was reassuring to me that they felt confident enough in Faith's progress to visit. That they weren't distancing themselves.

Meera looked to Karen, who I guess she must have decided was the more even-keeled of the two of us. "The white blood cell count came back and it was high, but that just confirms things."

After the hospital, Karen and I picked Andrew up and headed to church. Everything that was said there seemed to pertain directly to us. Giving thanks for what we had, for God's blessings, for His caring about us. And especially for our daughter who was somehow still with us.

We went over to my parents' house at about noon. The white tablecloth my family always uses at holidays made its semiannual appearance. We were all there as usual too: my sisters, Dorothy and Jane; my father and mother; and Karen, Andrew, and me.

The day was cool but sunny, with football games on TV and newspapers scattered about. We heard my mother's call to eat and climbed out of sofas and comfy chairs to assemble in our usual places around the dinner table before we could be scolded about food drying out due to latecomers.

As we seated ourselves and adjusted the crisp white napkins on our laps, everyone glanced round and began to recite grace as if on cue. My family did not pray out loud except in church or blessings at meals, and then only reciting the usual well-rehearsed prayers. But on this Thanksgiving Day, I felt compelled to do just a bit more. When everyone finished the usual litany, I slipped my words in before they could close: "And thank you, God, that Faith is with us this day."

No one looked up. No one said a word except "Amen." Forks moved and food was passed while the buzz of familiar family conversation resumed.

Later in the afternoon, Karen and I drove back to the hospital where with Faith and the NICU staff we celebrated our first Thanksgiving together. There were cardboard turkeys and cornstalks taped up on the walls and plenty of cookies, pies, and cakes spread around.

Faith looked peaceful. She slept through the entire visit. No one mentioned the infection, and the mood was so upbeat, I wasn't going to bring it up again. The infection was caught. It was being treated. She looked good. She had been with us for eighteen days. I'd never before in my life had so much to be thankful for.

•••

It was nice to have that Friday after Thanksgiving off from school. Karen brought Andrew to his playgroup while I did my morning hospital visit. She was very deliberate in making sure that even though she was sometimes at the hospital a couple of times a day, Andrew still went to his playgroup and YMCA classes and received the attention he needed.

"How's she doing?" I asked the nurse on duty. It was Cindy, the young ponytailed nurse. I was hoping to hear her say definitively, "The infection is under control."

Instead, she said, "Well, her CO_2 is kind of high. The doctors are thinking about a transfusion."

I thought you only got transfusions if you had lost a lot of blood. This didn't sound good. I wondered if it could be a sign that the infection was gaining a hold. "Oh. How does that help?" I asked.

Cindy hesitated. She appeared nervous. "Um. I'll get Dr. Aragones. She can explain it to you."

Dr. Aragones walked over a few minutes later, smiled politely, and explained, "Preemies of Faith's gestation often are unable to manufacture enough red blood cells for their needs. These blood cells carry oxygen throughout the bloodstream. It's important to keep oxygen saturation high, so to help this process, and boost red blood cells, sometimes a blood transfusion is used."

"Is this because of the infection?"

She dipped her head slightly. "Well. This is typical for most preemies."

So maybe, maybe not. That's as far as Dr. Aragones was willing to go. After Dr. Aragones left, Cindy said, "You might be able to donate blood directly to her. I'll get you the number for the blood bank. You can explain your situation to them."

I called the blood bank that afternoon to see about it, but found out that wasn't possible. The person on the phone reassured me, however, that "these babies get the best blood." That was an interesting thought, that some blood was better than other blood.

The transfusion was done on Saturday. We didn't see it happening, which was probably a good thing. Beth was on duty when we arrived in the afternoon. Karen got to ask the "How's she doing?"

Beth seemed pleased. "She's actually showing a good response. Her red count is better."

I felt my breath escape.

I hadn't realized I'd been holding it.

CHAPTER 23

Empty

I was hustling all around my classroom. Slicing bagels. Pouring juice into plastic cups. Filling trays with donuts. It was Monday morning. The last day of November. Day 22 for Faith and also the day of my class's annual poetry breakfast. In one hour my students would be entertaining their parents and families with our favorite poems and then sharing a quick breakfast together. It was a great way to channel all that post-Thanksgiving excitement.

Melanie Faulkner popped her head in my room. "Hey, how are you? How's Faith?" she asked.

"We're good. Thanks."

"So glad to hear that. Hey, I wanted to let you know that we have some prayer circles praying for her. My mom has one down in Alabama, and our friends near Boston do, and we have a local one here at our church too."

I'd never heard of a prayer circle before, but it sounded good. It felt powerful to know that groups of people in all those different places were praying for my daughter. "Thanks, Mel. That's great." I gave her a hug.

I got home from school around 5:00 and Karen met me at the door. I was excited to tell her about the prayer circles, but first I needed to hear how Faith was doing. I was hoping to hear some good news about the infection. We kissed and I asked, "How was your visit today?"

She said, "Oh, I wasn't able to make it. I got really busy with Andrew and had to go grocery shopping."

I took a deep breath, and though I didn't immediately say anything, I'm sure my demeanor revealed my feelings. I never wanted either of us to miss an opportunity to visit Faith. Karen, on the other hand, didn't feel this same compulsion. She was comfortable seeing Faith when she could and trusting, very rationally, that Faith would still be well cared for by the nurses and doctors even if we were not there.

When I went in for a visit, I wanted numbers. Karen was more big-picture oriented. Often she would keep notes, but she wasn't compulsive like me. She would ask the nurses, "How's she doing?" and be content with "Good" or "Fine" as an answer.

This different approach to the daily visits held the potential for a blowup that would distance us at a time when we needed each other as never before. Fortunately, the gravity of the whole situation made us both even more aware to try and be careful, to take a step back and continue to care for each other and not push an issue or our own personal preferences too far. So instead of asking why she couldn't go, I asked, "And what did you buy?"

That evening we visited the NICU together. Meera greeted us by waving and proclaiming across the room, "Come see what a big girl she is. She is over a pound."

We hurried over. There it was on her chart—500 grams. Almost 50 grams over a pound. Finally. What a gain! Meera nodded confidently. "She just needed a little blood, that's all."

I was hesitant to ask, but I had to. "How's the infection?"

Meera rewarded me with that same disdainful look I now expected and said, "She is doing good." She favored Karen with a big smile. "Thanks to Mommy's milk."

Along with the "best blood," Faith was also getting the "best milk." We had rented an electric breast pump and now Karen was busy with two daily sessions of pumping and freezing milk. Each evening we would now walk into the NICU with our pink-and-white cooler full of breast milk packets and into the freezer they'd go. The nurses were able to use them in part with the gavage feeding. Karen was feeding Faith. In a roundabout way, but still...

Encouraged by the weight gain, on Tuesday morning, the first of December, Dr. Aragones informed me, "I am going to move Faith's rate down from thirty to twenty-two." This was a very significant reduction in the machine-assisted breaths. It was awesome news.

That night we went in and met with the nurse on duty. "What's Faith's rate now?" I asked.

"Thirty," she said.

I must have reacted somehow because she quickly explained, "She was able to stay at twenty-two for a while, but she stopped tolerating her feedings."

"Oh," I mumbled. "I see."

She smiled and offered, "That's still really good. You know what they say. One step forward, two steps back? She's getting there though."

She was right, of course. But Dr. Hecht had originally said she hoped to get Faith off the respirator within a couple of weeks. It was close to a month now.

The rest of the week simultaneously flew and crawled by. It seemed to take a long time to get to Friday, but when I looked back, it was a blur. I saw Dr. Aragones in the morning. "How's the infection?" was my immediate question following our greetings, and had been all week.

In what sounded like a reluctant admission, Dr. Aragones answered, "She still has to finish her antibiotic, but it looks like it was caught early, before it could take hold and weaken her system."

If Dr. Aragones said something that positive and straightforward, then Faith must really and truly be past the infection. I thought immediately of Pam. Knowing our baby so intimately and her quick response had most likely saved Faith's life.

It was fantastic news. Karen and I hugged and chatted happily all the way to the car. Karen said, "What do you think about telling Andrew he has a little sister?"

We were a long way from being sure that he would ever see her, but it felt right to me too. Up to this point, we had told him we were going to the hospital to see the doctors, which was at least partly true and a reason he seemed to find perfectly acceptable.

After dinner, we went into our family room and I flopped down on the big old green couch. It was a hand-me-down from Karen's mom, worn and stained in a few places, but solid and low. Low enough for kids to climb up on and solid enough to withstand being used as a trampoline. I plopped Andrew down on my lap. It was easy to have a conversation with him even though he was only two and a half.

"Andrew?"

"Yeah, Dad?"

"I want to tell you something. You know how Mommy and Daddy have been going to the hospital a lot?"

He looked at me earnestly with his big brown eyes. "Uh-huh."

"Well, the reason we're going is because you have a baby sister in the hospital that the doctors and nurses are taking care of."

"Really? I have a sister?" He looked up, his eyes widening slightly.

"Yep."

"Why is she in the hospital?"

"Well, she's pretty small and weak, so she needs a lot of help from the doctors and nurses."

He pondered that for a second, then asked, "What's her name?"

"Faith."

He paused again. "Will I see her?"

"Yeah, sometime soon."

"Okay. Can I watch *Beauty and the Beast*?"

•••

After a quiet, uneventful weekend, Faith's fourth Monday, December 7, arrived.

Karen and I visited that evening and scrubbed up thoroughly as usual. We were definitely not going to be the ones to bring any germs into the NICU if we could help it. Karen put her milk packets in the freezer and then we walked into the main room. My compulsive, pessimistic brain continued to encourage me with thoughts like, Is she actually, *really* past the infection though? What if she relapses? She must be weakened and even more susceptible to something worse now.

I had to deliberately stop my thoughts and pray my new refrain once again: *Lord, I believe. Help me with my unbelief.* As we entered, our eyes moved routinely to Faith's warmer.

It was dark.

And it was empty.

CHAPTER 24

New Place

Where was she? What happened? I spun around scanning the room till I spotted Beth leaning against the far wall, watching us with an amused look on her face. She called over, "Want to see her new apartment?" She casually gestured to an Isolette next to her.

Karen and I flew across the floor. Faith was in the Isolette, covered snugly by her yellow blanket. "Oh my!" Karen exclaimed.

"Yeah," Beth said. "She was ready for her own place."

Karen and I laughed in relief.

Beth laughed too. "Isn't this great? We all figured it was time. She doesn't need to be worked on as much now."

"That's amazing," I said, beaming.

Beth continued, "Yeah. This is going to help prevent her from drying out and losing water weight. And it'll be quieter too, so less stressful on her system." She began pointing out the features of the Isolette like a real estate agent. She touched a panel on the front. "These dials are used to control the air temperature inside. And you can open the top or reach in through these little portholes."

Karen pointed to a couple of simple black-and-white pictures of a clown and a ball taped on the back wall. "What are those?" she asked.

"Those are stimulation pictures. They're used to help in the baby's cognitive development. And she's still got her water bed, of course." She plunked it playfully.

I was happily surprised to hear that they were thinking about Faith's cognitive development. It was that same positive, future-oriented outlook again, not just about surviving today.

Karen and I pulled up a couple of stools. Beth closed the top and unlatched one of the portholes. "Here. Let's open these." She unlatched the other one. "One for each parent," she said with a laugh.

We sat staring at the tiny sleeping figure. Karen shared her relief, whispering to me, "It just makes everything more normal."

Talk about perspective. We now considered babies in Isolettes "normal."

I started talking to Faith through the porthole. "Congratulations, sweetie. Good going." I reached in and touched her tiny hand. Her skin was warm and soft and moist. Her blue eyes fluttered open. They seemed to sparkle.

Karen cautiously touched Faith with a finger through the other porthole. "Nice place you have here, Faith. Remember, now. Keep gaining weight."

I rejoiced! Past the infection, out of the warmer, and headed for winter.

•••

In early September of 1983, if you'd happened to be in front of King's Cross Station in London on a crisp, bright Saturday morning, you might have noticed two twenty-something teachers from New Jersey clambering excitedly up the steps of a double-decker bus. That would have been me and Karen.

We had been teaching at our first overseas posts at the American School of Aberdeen, Scotland, for just a month and had decided to celebrate our first holiday weekend with an overnight sleeper train trip to London.

The air was sharp and chilly, but the sun was shining so it made the red bus look as if it had been freshly painted that morning. We sat on top so we wouldn't miss a thing. The bus pulled away, winding slowly through the streets on the way to our hotel. We drove by curving rows of beautiful old chalk-white buildings. Emerald-green parks and lush trees dotted the spaces between.

Growing up, I had been a big fan of anything British—James Bond, the Beatles, Monty Python, even the fish and chips we would get at the local Arthur Treacher's in New Jersey. Now here I was, in the heart of the real London for the first time. It was a dream come true.

A month later our school flew us to a weeklong teachers' conference at a four-star hotel in Rome. The Rome. With the Colosseum, the monuments, the art, and that incredibly delicious, cheap Italian food everywhere. We followed that later in the fall with a train and ferry to France for a weekend in Paris. In February, we went on a school-sponsored ski trip to the French Alps.

Over the next six years of teaching overseas, we spent several summers in Spain on the beach in Mallorca. We went hiking in the Black Forest in Germany. Cross-country skiing in Austria. Even a photo safari in Kenya. We had great jobs, tax-free salaries, incredible travel, and good health. We were only in our early thirties and we were set.

And was God part of this good life as I had constructed it? Not really. Looking back, I realize I had assigned Him a neat pocket, a tiny percentage of time and money that didn't require much thought or effort. I went to church. I prayed. I would throw a five in the collection basket most weeks. I tried to live morally. God was an underlying current in my life, one that had been there since I was a child.

There was one exception, though, during our second year teaching in Riyadh, Saudi Arabia. We were driving on the outskirts of the city on a large six-lane highway bordered on both sides by seemingly infinite stretches of brown sand and beige walled suburbs.

We were listening to some new tapes we had bought that day and chatting when I casually glanced out my driver-side window into an enormous truck tire bearing down on us.

I threw the steering wheel hard to the right. A massive tanker truck roared past into our lane, just missing us, but I lost control of the car and we careened into a guardrail at sixty miles an hour.

The impact whipped the back of the car around so I was slammed into my door, even with my seat belt on. A guardrail post came smashing through the window behind me, spraying us with pellets of glass. I yelled and clung to the wheel.

The car kept spinning. I felt back muscles rip and yelped in pain. We were now facing the wrong way on the highway, arcing across the lane. A white sedan was headed straight for us. It was going to be a head-on collision at highway speed. I roared in fear. My only thought in that moment was, no! Please, not yet! It was a straight-from-the-heart-to-God plea.

I cringed awaiting impact. Tires screeched and our dizzying sweep brought us smashing back into the guardrail again. The car rocked to a stop in a cloud of dust. Then silence. My heart was racing. We were facing the way we'd started. We had gone completely around 360 degrees twice. And the white car had somehow impossibly missed us.

I looked at Karen. She was pale and staring. Her eyes wide. I croaked, "Are you all right?"

She spoke slowly. "I'm fine. Are you okay?"

I didn't see any blood. I could move everything. "Yeah. I think so." My lower back hurt in a very weird way, though, and I knew you weren't supposed to move around with a back injury so I pried my door open and lay right down on the ground. Sirens began to wail.

Lying there on the ground, pebbles of glass all around me, I gazed up at our smashed and dented car. There was no way we could have missed the white sedan. No way. I looked up at the vast blue sky and prayed, *Thank you, Lord. Thank you.*

At the hospital, they found I had a minor compression of a vertebra and some small pieces of glass in my scalp. Karen had a small cut on her foot. Our fellow teachers who saw the car on its way to the junkyard couldn't believe we were walking.

It was a miracle. I had begged for more time and God had protected me. I don't remember specifically promising Him anything in return, but I know I was praying more in the imme-diate aftermath, thanking Him for saving me. But in a month or two, after I healed, I was back to work, doing my daily routine. I gradually, unthinkingly, returned God to His little pocket.

This time, though, with Faith, it wasn't a split-second "Please save me!" situation and then over. It was slower, more deliberate. It was constant. It forced me to come to God in prayer every day, every hour.

I was to the point now where I genuinely wanted to learn more about God. Not from a feeling of obligation or to check off a box, or so I could get into Heaven, but because He had become very real to me. That cold night driving from the hospital when I tuned into WCHR for the first time had started me listening to Christian radio and learning about modern Christian thinkers like Ravi Zacharias and classic Christian writers like C. S. Lewis. None of my family or friends knew who these people were. They were never mentioned in school, or in the papers, or on TV, or even in church. But now I knew.

On my second trip to Lamplighter Books, I bought James Dobson's *When God Doesn't Make Sense*. The title made me think of *When Bad Things Happen to Good People*. I got home and read it in one night. I was full of questions. The book contained many of these same questions and answers. When asked about how God could allow suffering and pain, Dobson answered in part, "As long as what happens to me is within the perfect will of the Father, I have no reason to fear—even if it costs me my life. It is an article of faith that we can trust Him to do what is best even if it appears contrary to our own wishes or the prevailing attitudes of the day."

It was a hard truth, but it was just what Tony Evans had said. What I wanted, my will, even if it was requesting something as innately good as saving the life of an infant, might not be according to God's plan. God was in control. And He would guide me if I came to Him and asked. So I did. I kept asking and asking and asking.

And God was answering.

CHAPTER 25

Dr. Bernard

December 7 may have been a day that lived in infamy in US history, but for us it was a huge milestone. Dr. Aragones came over when she spotted us with Beth at the Isolette. We stood up and greeted her. She smiled. "She looks good there, ys?"

If Dr. Aragones was smiling, we must be making real progress here, I thought. I pulled over a stool for her while Karen replied, "She looks great there."

Dr. Aragones nodded and sat down. Then she said, "But you know, we are still experiencing difficulties in maintaining Faith's IV properly."

I knew what she meant. I had seen nurses take many tries to find an IV site that would work and get it established, only to have it "blow out" within the hour. Recently, we had come in for a visit to find the IV sticking out of the top of Faith's head.

Dr. Aragones shifted on the stool. "I would like to plan to put a long line in Faith as soon as we can. You remember she had a long line inserted almost immediately after birth when she was brought into the NICU for the first time. It was removed after only a few days."

"I do remember that, yes," Karen replied.

"Well, this new long line will be inserted into the chest through the shoulder and will replace the constant need for new IV sites. This is the best thing to do and will allow Faith less strain and more efficient delivery of medicines and anything else she might need."

I didn't like the mental picture of a tube going into Faith's chest. This sounded like a step backward to me. "There's no way to avoid this then?" I asked.

She tilted her head and shrugged slightly. Almost apologetically, she said, "Well, of course, it doesn't have to be done right away. We could wait and keep trying to find IV sites, but this is what I recommend for the reasons I gave you. You can think about it and we can talk more tomorrow."

Dr. Aragones folded her small hands neatly in her lap. "I also wanted to let you know that I am going on a two-week leave." Her voice got even smaller. "I've finished my shift here and am going home to Florida tomorrow night to see my family."

I had never thought about her home situation, being a thousand miles away from her family for two to four weeks at a time. "You probably can't wait," Karen said.

"Yes. I am anxious to see my girls." She paused and then added, "They are teenagers."

We all laughed at that, picturing what teenage girls might get up to without Mom around. She nodded and smiled again. "So you will get to meet Dr. Bernard," she said in her little voice. "She is very good," she added.

We talked a bit more about her two teenage daughters and then Dr. Aragones left. I glanced down at Faith to say a goodbye as we prepared to leave. I touched the top of her head with my finger. She was curled peacefully on her side, oblivious to all the action around her. I sat there wondering what the new doctor would be like.

A nurse came over. Glancing down at Faith, she said, "Congratulations on the move."

Karen and I gave her a big smile and said, "Yeah. Thanks." I stood. "I hear a new neonatologist is coming in. Dr. Bernard?"

With kind of a funny lilt in her voice, she said, "Oh yes."

"Have you worked with her?" Karen asked.

"Yep. A little."

That was all she was giving us. I could tell I was going to have to ask the direct question. "How is she?"

The nurse glanced up at the ceiling as if searching for the right words. "She's very...bright. Young, but very competent."

I felt my shoulders relax, then she added, "She's maybe a little different than the other doctors."

"Really?" I asked.

She was walking away. "Yeah. You'll see."

Leaving the hospital that night, Karen and I hustled across the parking lot, our bodies bent against the December wind. We hopped in the car, hurriedly slamming doors against the frigid cold. Mercifully, after a few blocks the heat kicked in and filled the front seat. It was now warm enough for me to collect my thoughts. I asked Karen, "So what do you think about this long line?"

"Well," she replied. "It sounds like she needs it."

I was feeling apprehensive about the whole thing and

countered, "It looks like she's doing all right without it though."

Karen shook her head slightly. "I don't know. Maybe it's not a big deal."

We drove a couple more blocks in silence. "Yeah," I finally said. "Everything Dr. Aragones says makes sense. It's just surgery..."

The word *surgery* hung there in the air.

"They already did it once when she was born," Karen replied. "And she was weaker then."

"I know," I said. "You're right." In the back of my mind, even though I dreaded the thought of it, I already knew that I would agree. I just wanted to talk it through a little. By this point, I had come to trust Dr. Aragones because, basically, she had kept Faith alive.

The next morning when I went in, there were pieces of paper all over Faith's Isolette. I was thinking, What the heck is this? Then when I got close enough, I realized what was going on. HAPPY 1 MONTH BIRTHDAY! HAPPY BIRTHDAY, FAITH! GOOD GOING! They were handwritten notes and cards, all made by the nurses. December 8. It never occurred to me to mark it as a sort of birthday.

Dr. Aragones appeared. She pulled her mask down, held out a clipboard, and said, "I have the papers here for the long line if you would like to sign. Or we could do it later."

"No. This is fine," I said and immediately took the pen she offered and signed. "Karen and I talked about it."

She nodded, smiled her polite smile, and said, "I will schedule it. Probably soon. Even though I will be away, someone will take care of it."

So it was going to happen.

The next evening, Karen and I were standing beside Faith's Isolette when a woman in a neatly pressed white doctor's coat came striding over. She was small and thin, with long, wiry black hair neatly pulled back. "Mr. and Mrs. Krech?" She stuck her hand out at a straight ninety-degree angle from her body and announced, "It's nice to meet you. I'm Dr. Bernard." She had intense dark eyes and sharp features. She looked directly at us and held that eye contact as she spoke.

Dr. Bernard's voice had a lot of energy behind it. "So, Faith is critical, but stable. She's made a lot of progress. But she still has a way to go." We nodded agreement. "Could we chat a bit?" she asked.

"Sure," we replied.

"Please have a seat." She pointed to a couple of stools. As we sat, she stood right in front of us. "I've heard from my colleagues about your daughter and read through the records. Now I'd like to hear from you."

"Of course. Whatever you need," Karen said.

"You, the parents, know your baby better than anyone else," she continued. "You may notice things even staff might not."

Karen and I agreed that no one knew the babies better than the nurses, but I appreciated that Dr. Bernard wanted to hear from us too.

"So, would you care to tell me a bit about Faith's birth and your experience so far?"

Karen and I took turns recounting all the events of the last month and then Dr. Bernard asked us a string of questions. Did we notice anything that seemed to bother Faith? Was there anything Faith seemed to like? How were our visits? How often did we visit? Were we happy with her care?

At the end of the interview, Dr. Bernard shook hands again. "Thank you for your time," she said in a businesslike manner. She moved off with quick, purposeful steps. She was impressive, and obviously cared about how things were going.

In our fifteen or so minutes of conversation, though, she hadn't once mentioned the long line, and I didn't bring it up because, frankly, I had the juvenile hope that somehow the issue might just simply fade away. Realistically, though, I figured it might take a day or two as Dr. Bernard settled in.

For the rest of the week, Faith steadily, though incrementally, improved on her oxygen needs and her weight. We met daily with Dr. Bernard, but she never mentioned the long line. Neither did we. Finally, on Friday I reluctantly brought it up. "Dr. Bernard, before Dr. Aragones left, she had us sign for a long line insertion on Faith. Has that been scheduled?" I asked.

"No." Her answer was immediate and blunt. "I have no intention of inserting the line. We will have to make do with the IV sites."

I paused. I hadn't expected that. I'd tried not to question the doctors' decisions any more than I absolutely felt I had to, but this was major. "Well, Dr. Aragones seemed to think the long line was a necessity." Dr. Bernard said nothing. I followed up as politely as I could, "Why the change then?"

She folded her hands behind her back. "There is a very significant risk of infection with a *piece of plastic* being inserted deep into Faith's system and in constant contact with the outside world."

She said "piece of plastic" like you would say "piece of excrement." The same level of derision.

She continued in a sharp, clipped delivery, "We have an overwhelming need here to guard against further infection. That is our priority. A long line would run counter to that."

It made sense. "I see."

She added pointedly, "And there is no way I plan on taking that kind of risk with this baby."

For me, with anything else in the rest of my life, that would have been enough. I am not a confrontational person. But this was Faith, and I needed 100 percent confirmation that this was the right thing. So I pursued it a little further, saying, "Well, Dr. Aragones felt that constantly finding IV sites was too stressful on Faith's system."

Dr. Bernard replied instantly, without a flicker of change in her expression, "Yes, there are lots of ways to look at it, but this is my view."

And she was now the neonatologist in charge, at least for the next few weeks. "Okay," I said. "We appreciate it."

"You're very welcome," she said. She spun on her heel and was off to the next baby.

I was relieved. No long line. But little did I know that Dr. Bernard would soon be helping us through an even riskier situation.

CHAPTER 26

The Valve

Our first week with Dr. Bernard had gone really well. We were basking in the relief of the long-line decision, and Faith was taking in the predigested food and breast milk and starting to gain weight—grams at a time, but moving in the right direction. Dr. Bernard was there on Sunday, and I greeted her with my usual "How's Faith doing?"

Dr. Bernard always seemed to be moving, even when she was standing still. As she spoke, though, she focused her energy directly on you. "She's stable, yes," she answered. "But we have a problem developing." She glanced down at her clipboard, flipping quickly through a few pages and looking intently at something there. "Faith's blood count shows she is too high in phosphorus."

I could feel my body tighten in response. I had learned from Dr. Aragones that too much potassium was deadly. No doubt too much phosphorus was going to be significantly bad news as well.

Dr. Bernard paused to check that we were following her. Karen and I responded with silent nods. "There could be various reasons for this, but I suspect it's due to what is called a patent ductus. This is basically a heart valve that has not fully closed."

Karen and I exchanged a worried glance.

"I'm going to schedule an echocardiogram," Dr. Bernard continued. "That will provide a record of the blood flow in and around the heart. We should then know if we're looking at a valve problem or not."

My next thought was irrational and full of denial. How could they tell just from looking at a blood sample with a little too much phosphorus that she had a heart valve problem? Nothing like this had been mentioned before by anyone. However, it sounded like a simple test, and hopefully it would prove Dr. Bernard's suspicions wrong. Karen and I agreed.

"When would you do this?" Karen asked.

Dr. Bernard replied, "Tomorrow afternoon."

"I can be there," Karen said.

•••

Monday morning, December 13, I was back in the NICU at 7:00 a.m. when I saw Red-Haired Debbie. "What's up, Debbie?" I greeted her.

"Well, Dad," she said, "the good news is that Faith's rate has been moved down to eighteen, and her oxygen is only thirty percent. Woo-hoo!" Then she held up a tiny tube of cream. "But she's got a fungal rash on her abdomen. Hopefully this antibiotic will stop it from spreading. Gotta watch these little things."

I was acutely aware that seemingly little things like a rash could balloon into disasters. It was something new to worry about along with the valve. I had to catch myself and try and turn a worry into a prayer.

Karen was there in the afternoon when the echocardiogram

was done. She watched with some distress as the Isolette was opened and Faith was lifted out and placed onto a tray. It took the technicians several attempts, with Faith exposed to the open air and struggling, before they got a satisfactory reading.

As they were packing up their equipment, Karen asked the technicians, "How did it look?"

One of the them replied, "Well, we finally got a good enough reading, but we have to send it out."

"Could you tell anything yet?"

She said, "No. We'll have to see."

Karen said a couple of the nurses were shaking their heads at what Faith had to go through to get that reading.

The next day's weigh-in revealed that Faith had dropped 30 grams—we all assumed from the strain of the test. Karen asked Debbie, "Any word on the echocardiogram?"

Debbie shrugged. "The early, unofficial word is that they couldn't tell. They sent the tape to a pediatric cardiologist at another hospital for his interpretation." Debbie, apparently sensing Karen's concern, smiled broadly and said heartily, "Hey. She had an excellent blood gas and no bradys today."

"That's good to hear," Karen said.

"Real good for me. I like it when our girl keeps breathing, ha, ha." Debbie reported further, "Her rate is good too. Eighteen breaths a minute with oxygen at only twenty-one percent. That's almost room-air."

This was terrific. It sounded like Faith was finally moving toward getting off the respirator. I concluded that there couldn't be a valve problem with this kind of progress. I allowed myself to relax a little.

Encouraged by an excellent blood gas, Dr. Bernard ordered Faith's rate dropped down to sixteen while her oxygen remained in the mid-twenties. Faith responded with a blood gas that was not so good, and the rate went back up to eighteen by the evening. When I nervously asked Suzie about this, she replied, "She's just letting everyone know 'Not yet, folks.'"

That evening, Dr. Bernard met with us as usual. She stood straight in her white coat. "We heard from the pediatric cardiologist. He has examined the echocardiogram. In his opinion, there is an open valve, and it will have to be closed."

My mind raced to the frightening, inevitable conclusion—heart surgery. On a child this tiny. How would that even be possible?

Dr. Bernard continued, "First of all, surgery will probably not be necessary." She pressed her clipboard to her chest. "Instead, we would like to try a drug called Indocin. The chemical effect of the drug is designed to close the valve without any other intervention."

No surgery. What a relief. But then Dr. Bernard shared the flip side. "Indocin, however, is very strong and has potential side effects. It can cause decreased urine output, lowered feeding tolerance, and gastrointestinal bleeding or other forms of internal bleeding."

Dr. Aragones had warned us about brain bleeds. How they could result in cerebral palsy, blindness, or loss of body functions. I seesawed back to my recently vacated full-blown fear again.

"These side effects occur in a small number of cases, but they are possibilities," she said. "Still, this is our best option, and I highly recommend we pursue this course." Dr. Bernard handed us the clipboard with a small sheaf of papers on top. "I will need your permission to administer the drug. You'll have to sign the consent form and then we can go ahead. But of course, take as much time as you need to think about it."

Karen regrouped enough to ask a question. "Is it possible that the valve will eventually close on its own as she grows more?"

"She seems to be making good progress," I suggested hopefully.

"No. That would not be a realistic option," she answered firmly. "The problem would only get worse, and we need to move on it as soon as possible."

I knew Dr. Bernard wasn't going to perform any unnecessary procedures. That was clear from her decision with the long line. Karen and I exchanged a nod. This was obviously something we were going to have to do. Karen said, "Yes. We'll sign."

As Karen passed me the clipboard, Dr. Bernard said, "The Indocin will be administered in three doses at twelve-to-twenty-four-hour intervals. We'll give her the first dose tonight."

We shook hands and parted. It was time to add some new lines to our prayers.

•••

In my classroom on Thursday morning, I sat at my desk in the quiet before school started. *Please help the Indocin work. Help it not to hurt her*, I prayed. I kept that mantra/prayer going the rest of the day in the back of my mind.

During lulls in the classroom action, I pictured what the drug was doing in Faith's body. I visualized her heart with a small hole slowly closing. When I got home from work, Karen greeted me at the door. She told me immediately what I was hoping to hear. "The morning's blood test came back fine. No negative effects from the drug!"

We hugged.

My mother was there to watch Andrew that night. I didn't mention the Indocin situation. I didn't want everyone worrying about every single thing that came up.

When we got to the hospital, we found Dr. Hecht on duty. I was always glad to see her. I smiled as I approached and said, "I heard the first dose of Indocin went okay."

"Yes. She did fine. We're going to give her the second dose later tonight."

I assumed the effect of the drug must be cumulative, that this next dose would continue the job the first dose began but also be riskier. I prayed again. I saw the hole closing. I prayed, *Keep her safe.*

On my Friday morning visit, everything was quiet around Faith's Isolette. She was sleeping. I checked with Dark-Haired Debbie and asked for probably the two-hundredth time, "How's she doing?"

She knew exactly what my concern was. "She's doing fine. Her stool sample showed no blood, and blood samples revealed normal platelets."

"That's great to hear," I said.

Debbie never got too excited. She just stated the facts. "Yes. She's doing well. She's handling the Indocin okay."

That was just the reassurance I needed. I told Karen the news at breakfast. "That's so good," she said and hugged me.

"Thank God," I said.

"Oh yes," she echoed. "Thank God."

Andrew joined in. "Thank God!" he added.

Karen smiled and hugged him. She said, "I'm taking Andrew to Tumble Tots today at the Y and then we've got Steven and Lisa's Christmas party tonight."

"Oh yeah. That's right. We can go to the hospital early." Things outside of hospital, home, and school were not much on my radar at all.

That night, Karen and I found Dr. Syed making the rounds. I was glad to see him. He was always so confident and positive about Faith. "How's everything?" I asked.

"She is doing fine," he answered. "You are just in time. I am going to be checking on the valve now."

He opened the top of the Isolette, bent down, and moved the stethoscope around Faith's chest. He kept at it for what felt to me like an hour, this huge man contorting himself this way and that over this tiny baby. Finally, he straightened up and faced us.

"I believe the valve is closed," he said. "I am going to call Dr. Bernard."

He retreated to the nurses' station and got on the phone. We waited. It seemed to be taking an unusually long time. Maybe Dr. Bernard would insist on the next dose to be sure. Maybe she would want to check it herself. Finally, he walked back into the room. "The third dose of Indocin will not be necessary," he announced with a smile.

Faith had tolerated the Indocin and her valve had closed. Her "quality" makeup, as Dr. Syed liked to say, had helped her over another hurdle. And maybe some of those prayers made a difference too.

CHAPTER 27

Phone Call

Karen and I walked back to the car holding gloved hands as the wind whipped around the parking lot. Karen snuggled into me. We were headed to her brother's Christmas party with very positive news. "You know what I think we should do?" she asked.

"What?" I asked.

"Send out a birth announcement," she said simply.

It was almost the end of December, but we hadn't even once talked about a formal announcement, I guess because we didn't know what was going to happen. We still didn't know, but there was a real and growing hope that neither of us voiced aloud: God was going to save Faith.

She now weighed 1 pound and 3.8 ounces, or 560 grams, a fact we decided to leave off the announcements.

•••

The next evening as we entered the NICU we saw a cluster of nurses in their white, pink, and blue scrubs hovering close to Faith's Isolette, and eyeing us as we entered. We knew that look by now. Something was up.

Karen got to the Isolette first. "She's wearing a shirt!" she exclaimed.

The group cheered and clapped.

Peering over Karen's shoulder, I saw our daughter wearing what looked like a little nightgown. She had always been just totally naked from Day 1 so it was quite a different look. Suzie explained, "It's supposed to be a T-shirt for your regular-size preemie. So of course, with our girl, it covers her down to the ankles."

Faith had never been allowed to wear anything before because it would have interfered with the need for constant intervention. There was no problem with her getting cold because the nurses would just turn up the temperature in the Isolette, put a knit cap on her head, or cover her with a blanket. Faith's hat made her look like a miniscule hip-hop skateboarder.

As the other nurses moved back to their stations, Aunt Meera remained. She raised her eyebrows and nodded toward Faith. "You like her shirt?"

Then she quickly changed her tone and, in a voice dripping with mock disgust, said, "You see, we had to put it on her because of *him*." She pointed to the next Isolette. A tiny infant with a light blue cap on his head slept peacefully. "That's Eddie. He got here last night. We have to have some modesty now that she has a boyfriend right next door. We don't want him looking at her."

We laughed together, celebrating a small step toward normalcy—clothes. Well, at least a T-shirt.

We sat there by Faith's Isolette enjoying her new look as Dr. Hecht worked her way across the room. By this time, Dr. Hecht was one of my favorite people in the world. My anger with her on that first night was a long-distant memory. She had saved Faith's life, prayed for her, and she had done it despite her initial misgivings about trying at all. As she checked Faith and talked things over with Meera, I stood up.

When they finished, we stepped forward and shook her hand. "How's she doing?" I asked.

She grinned and said jauntily, "She's the healthiest person in the room. We should all be so healthy."

I chuckled. My heart was warmed. If anybody really knew how Faith was doing, it would be Dr. Hecht. After all, she had been there from the beginning.

Then on Tuesday, Faith's morning blood gas was not so good and another transfusion was ordered. This seemed to do the trick, though, as she continued to move her rate down throughout the day. Beth greeted me Wednesday morning with "She's down to a rate of ten. And oxygen at only twenty-five percent."

"Another new record," I replied. I felt my chest fill up with air. I was pumped.

Beth continued, "Ten breaths per minute. She's doing all the rest on her own. I'm thinking she's almost ready to get off the respirator."

"Really? That's terrific!"

"Yeah," she said with a grin. "Those transfusions are great stuff. I'm thinking about getting one myself."

I glanced at Faith's chart. She was up to a strapping 670 grams. She was getting bigger and stronger.

Later that day, though, a nurse who didn't smile a lot, which was rare among this group, was on duty. She was thin and small, with dyed-black hair pulled back severely in a tight ponytail. As I watched Faith, she worked around the Isolette, not speaking at all until finally she looked over at me. "You know Faith has a new infection," she said.

I drew back as if I'd been struck. This was the first I'd heard of it and she was talking about it as if it were common knowledge. All I could think to say was, "Really?"

"Yes. It's candida. It's a yeast infection in her mouth. There's been no yeast yet in the blood. We're treating her for it, but it's got to be watched."

"How are you treating her?" I asked.

She continued somberly, "We're giving her these drops. She probably got it from the breathing tube. We found some traces in her tracheal aspirations."

I kept hoping she would end her sentence with "but it's nothing" or "it'll be fine." But she didn't.

After school when I came home, Karen met me at the door as usual. We kissed and sat down on the couch together. Andrew ran over. "Hey, Dad," he called.

"Hey, Andrew." I grabbed him up on my lap and it took some effort. He was growing into a solid little guy with round cheeks and sturdy little legs. "How'd she do this afternoon?" I asked.

Karen reached in her pocket and pulled out a slip of paper. She read aloud, "Her rate is fifteen and oxygen is thirty percent."

I felt some tension in my chest. "This morning her rate was ten and the oxygen was only twenty-five percent."

"What are you guys talking about?" Andrew asked.

"Just hospital stuff," I said.

"Oh," he replied. He jumped off my lap and flew out of the room making a plane noise.

Karen shrugged. "That's not much of a change."

"This one nurse told me she has a new infection. Candida. They're giving her drops for it."

"Oh," Karen said.

"How was her weight?"

Karen looked at the paper again. "No change."

Her rate and oxygen ticking back up were not good signs, and this was right after a transfusion, which was supposed to make everything better. Plus no weight gain. I didn't have a good feeling about this.

That evening at about five o'clock, Karen and I were setting the table for dinner. Andrew was playing on the family room rug with his plastic army men. The phone rang. I picked it up and said hello.

"Hello, Mr. Krech. This is Pam from the NICU."

CHAPTER 28

Holding

This was how I had secretly pictured the worst possible news unfolding. It would be a phone call. The NICU had never called us at home before. My voice wobbled in reply, "Hi, Pam."

Karen was at the stove stirring something. She put the spoon down and stared. We only knew one Pam.

"What time will you be in tonight?" Pam asked.

"We were planning on coming in about six." I braced for impact. "Why?"

"Well, I was wondering if you might want to hold Faith."

Wait. Hold her? It took me a few seconds to comprehend this. Then a flood of relief washed over me, followed by excitement, followed closely by a different kind of fear. With some trepidation, I answered, "Absolutely." I gave Karen the okay sign.

Pam replied, "Good. I'll have her all ready at six. See you then."

Karen moved next to me as I hung up. "What is it?"

I explained, "We get to hold her tonight."

At six, Karen and I walked into the unit, scrubbed, and put on our gowns. Across the room, I could see Pam's short brown hair peeking over the back of the quilted rocking chair where she sat.

As we approached, she glanced over her shoulder. In a

nonchalant way, like she was talking to an old pal, she said, "Hey, Faith. Look who's here."

Faith was cradled snugly in Pam's arms, a yellow blanket tucked tight around her, a pink knit cap perched on her tiny head, her tubes and wires tethering her to the Isolette. It was so strange to see her out here in the open air. "Want to hold her?" Pam asked.

Karen and I smiled and mumbled, "Definitely, yeah."

Pam raised an eyebrow. "You sure about that?"

I chuckled and managed a "yup," but Faith looked miniscule out here right next to all the big people and machines.

"How about you first, Dad?" Pam suggested.

With all the false confidence I could muster, I replied, "Sounds good."

She stood up with Faith and I took her place in the rocker. I set my arms in position. I started thinking, don't drop her, don't squeeze her, don't pull any wires off, get your hands set. The room began to feel warm.

Pam lowered Faith into my arms. She was literally as light as a kitten. I gently cradled her as she stared up at me, her big blue eyes unblinking.

I had held Andrew for what seemed like months on end during his first year, but after only a few minutes of holding Faith, my arms began to ache. Sweat dampened my shirt. Faith continued to stare. She was very still.

After at most five minutes, I forced a smile, looked to Karen, and asked, "Would you like a turn?"

She smiled back and we carefully switched over. I stood up and stretched my frozen joints. Pam remained alongside. She glanced at the respirator numbers. "We'll see how she tolerates it. If she has any problems, we'll put her back in."

Meanwhile, two other nurses strolled over to check out the scene. Then Beth appeared with the Polaroid camera. "Say cheese," she called out as she snapped a couple of pictures.

After Karen had her few minutes, Pam said, "Let's put her back in." She took Faith and quickly and smoothly deposited her back in the Isolette. She studied Faith's readings again. "She liked it," she said and winked. "Little early Christmas present for you two."

We smiled till I'm sure you could've seen our back molars. The fact that Pam felt Faith was strong enough to visit outside the Isolette came at just the right time. It gave me a badly needed confidence boost. We practically skipped through the parking lot to the car.

•••

Christmas Eve fell on a Thursday. Karen and I took Andrew to a local mall that morning to watch Santa arrive on his sled. It was a sunny, crisp, beautiful morning to be out and about. A crowd of smiling parents and cheering children greeted the huge reindeer and the jolly Santa as they entered the mall courtyard.

Andrew laughed and bounced in my arms. There was still a lot to do to get ready for Christmas Day, but we easily managed a visit that evening to see Faith. We didn't know the nurse on duty, but Karen wished her a merry Christmas and asked, "How's Faith?"

She smiled. "We've had to give her a little more oxygen, but she's doing fine."

"How are her numbers?" I asked.

"We've been able to keep her rate at fifteen, with oxygen between forty and fifty percent."

That was a significantly higher oxygen percentage. "Who's the doctor on duty?" I asked.

"Dr. Patel," she said. She paused. "I'll get him if you want to speak to him."

"I'd appreciate it. Thanks," I replied.

Dr. Patel was a young Indian neonatologist with coppery skin and neatly combed black hair. He was filling in from another hospital. I had only seen him once before. In a way, that made it easier to be more direct. After introducing myself, I got to the point. "Do you have any guesses about why Faith's oxygen needs are up?"

He shook his head slightly. "That is hard to say."

"Do you think it could be the yeast infection?"

"That's very speculative," he cautioned. "It's possible it might be the yeast, or perhaps a beginning of some stiffening of the lungs." I froze. "Then again, it may be simply that she is tired and needs to rest at a level where she has more assistance."

I'm sure the disappointment was all over my face. "Thanks," I said. I turned to leave. I began a feeble mental attempt to be deliberately positive and focus on all the good things of the season. I had so much to be thankful for, but Faith's breathing was weakening. Only a week before, Dr. Hecht had referred to her as the healthiest person in the room, and now she was going backward on the respirator.

The young doctor interrupted my thoughts. "You know, she is doing well. She is very stable on low vent support."

I stopped and looked back. His positive comments bounced right off my wall of worry. I said, "I'm a little concerned about her rate and oxygen percentage continuing to go up."

He smiled shyly and almost apologetically answered, "These are very low levels compared to previous levels."

I didn't reply. He seemed unsure whether to continue, but finally did. "She will get there. You have to give her time." He paused. "You know, you can't realistically expect her progress to be all up in a straight line." He shared this in a polite and gentle tone. Then he reached out, shook my hand, and said, "Merry Christmas."

I was completely and totally embarrassed. After all the little miracles. After all the incredible progress Faith had made. Even after holding her out in the open the other day. Here I was still weak and doubting and paranoid.

I used to mentally shake my head about the Jewish people in the Old Testament stories I heard in church. They witnessed miracle after miracle, the plagues on Pharaoh, crossing the Red Sea, and the manna from heaven, but they still doubted and then ignored God. What were they thinking? How obstinate were they? Well, I wasn't doing any better. When I finished up my visit, I went to the chapel. I prayed again with greater intent than ever: *Lord, I believe. Help me in my unbelief. Forgive me my unbelief.*

•••

On Christmas morning, Andrew came jumping down the stairs at dawn. He tore open his presents as only a two-year-old can. Within minutes, toys, boxes, wrapping paper, and pine needles blanketed the living room floor. We had fun, loving visits with our families after church. Before leaving our house for the hospital in the afternoon, I committed myself to not asking even once about oxygen levels. To just try and appreciate the fact that we were all together on Christmas—something that had seemed impossible the month before. I would focus on my blessings for a change, not the bad that might happen.

The NICU was in full holiday mode. Christmas lights and decorations hung along the walls. A brightly lit Christmas tree and a glowing menorah stood guard on either end of a table piled with presents. Holiday cards were strung across the bulletin boards. Dozens of them were photo cards of "graduates" of the NICU. Seeing them gave me an immediate lift.

We headed across the room toward Faith's Isolette, where a group of nurses hovered. "Merry Christmas," they called in unison.

"Merry Christmas," we called back. As we all exchanged hugs, I got a glimpse of Faith. She seemed somehow to be shining under the twinkling Christmas lights. As my eyes adjusted, I saw she was wearing a silky white dress with ruffled sleeves. It looked like an old-fashioned baptismal gown.

"Oh, how beautiful," Karen said. "Where is it from?"

Beth answered quickly, "She was out shopping this afternoon."

I had to laugh out loud. Then Kate, the nurse who had come in on her day off that first Saturday, raised her hand slightly. "I got it for her."

"Where did you find something like that?" Karen asked.

"Well, it is a doll's dress, but she is a living doll," she said with a laugh.

"It's great," Karen responded. She hugged Kate. "Thank you so much."

Kate hugged Karen back. "Well, a girl does like to wear something nice on Christmas, right?"

From what we had seen of Kate looking especially sharp in her own street clothes, she may have been projecting a little.

Faith had made it all the way to Christmas, and the staff had made sure she'd received her first ever Christmas present. Her still being with us was, of course, the best Christmas gift any of us could have ever asked for. And to top it all off, we were allowed to hold her again, this time with much less sweat and trepidation. Faith didn't move much at all. Just stared up with those big blue eyes as if to say, "And now what?"

Which was exactly what I was wondering.

CHAPTER 29

Seventy Percent

I had the week after Christmas off, so making time to visit the hospital was easier than ever. Karen and I went in together on Tuesday, the twenty-ninth, and Suzie greeted us. "Hey. I hear you guys are holding your little darling now. You up for that today?"

We weren't expecting the invitation, but there was no way we were going to turn down that kind of offer. Karen went first, nestling in the rocker as Suzie delicately placed Faith in her arms. Karen beamed.

"Looking good," Suzie said as she glanced over the monitors. She looked back to Karen and Faith. "You two are very natural together there."

"Thanks," Karen said. She smiled at Suzie. "I'm getting used to it."

Suzie had been the one from the beginning who said how important touch was to a preemie's health and development. I was thinking that holding and snuggling was the ultimate form of touch for a baby.

I looked at Faith's chart. She was 1 pound, 12.5 ounces. Edging toward 2 pounds. Though not anywhere near normal, it was way better than a pound. On the drive home, Karen and I decided it was finally time for Andrew to meet Faith.

I broached the subject with him that night after dinner. "Hey, big guy. You ready to go meet your little sister?"

He immediately answered, "Yep," hopped up out of his chair, walked into the hall, and took his coat off the hook.

"Tomorrow, buddy," I laughed. "Tomorrow."

He certainly appeared to be ready, but we still had some concern about how he would actually react once he saw Faith. However, the next day when we did all go, the whole situation at the hospital—doctors, lights, alarms, and incredibly tiny baby—did not appear to faze him in the least. As he gazed at her through the plastic walls of the incubator, Suzie asked, "What do you think of your little sister?"

"Her name is Faith," he responded.

"Oh, right, Faith," she answered. "What do you think of Faith?"

He kept looking. "She's good," he replied.

He kept his eyes on his sister, only glancing back at us now and then with a little grin on his face. Then Suzie asked, "Would you like to see some toys?"

"Yes, please," he answered and immediately abandoned Faith.

Suzie led him to the well-stocked sibling playroom and he was soon laying out a set of wooden train tracks while Karen and I took turns shuttling between brother and sister.

As the new year began, Andrew joined us as a regular visitor. On January 7, we all went in and saw Dr. Hecht on duty. When Karen asked how Faith was doing, she gave us all good news. "She's at a rate of only fourteen breaths per minute with oxygen back down to the high twenties. Her feedings have been increased, and her weight is now 2.2 pounds."

She was bouncing back.

Doctor Hecht continued, "To keep that weight gain going, we're alternating Faith's feedings between predigested formula and Karen's breast milk." We had noticed that the little frozen breast-milk packets that had been piling up in the NICU freezer were going fast, so Karen was still pumping a couple of times a day to meet demand. Then on the twelfth of January, we got our second phone call from the unit. I was in the family room and Karen was upstairs. I ran into the kitchen and grabbed the phone. "Hello?"

"This is Debbie from the NICU."

It was Dark-Haired Debbie. The serious Debbie. I responded with the same feeling of impending doom as the call from Pam. "Hi, Debbie," I said carefully.

"I'm just calling to say we have more good news," she said. "We got the order that Faith can begin 'big-girl feedings.'"

Relief washed over me once again. "Sounds good, Debbie, but what does that mean exactly?"

"Oh, sorry. It means she'll get individual larger feeds rather than a little bit each hour. We'll see how she tolerates it and let you know, but we all think she's ready. Just wanted to share the good news."

"Thank you. That was great that you called," I replied. "We appreciate it."

When we saw Debbie the next day, I immediately asked, "How'd the feeding go?"

"Her rate is down to eleven. That's almost nothing."

"What's her oxygen?" I asked.

She grinned. "Twenty-five percent."

"Super," I said.

Karen asked, "Is Dr. Bernard on?" We hadn't seen her over the Christmas break. It had been mostly Dr. Hecht and Dr. Syed, with the occasional visiting doctor. I had assumed that was because it was the holidays.

"Oh, Dr. Bernard has finished here. She won't be back. I don't think we'll see Dr. Aragones much longer either."

We were both surprised and a little sad. We never got to say goodbye or thank you. I would definitely miss Dr. Bernard. I had a lot of confidence in her. "So is the doctor situation changing for some reason?" I asked.

Debbie said, "The hospital administration is actively searching for a permanent director to replace Dr. Aragones and Dr. Bernard."

Karen asked hopefully, "Do you think it might be Dr. Hecht?"

She shook her head. "No. They already said it won't be any of the present neonatologists. It's going to be someone new."

Another new doctor. I wondered what he or she would be like.

I was back at work and Karen was taking care of Andrew, tutoring twice a week, and doing her freelance writing for ETS. As a Christmas gift, she had given me *The Joyful Christian* by C. S. Lewis, which I was reading every day. Until I heard Lewis quoted on Christian radio, I'd only known him as the author of the Narnia Chronicles, a classic fantasy series for children, and I only knew that from being an elementary school teacher. I had no idea he was one of the best known of all twentieth-century Christian thinkers and writers.

I was reading *The Joyful Christian* over the break and came upon a wonderful short piece called "What Are We to Make of Jesus Christ?" In it, Lewis talks about how a good many people are willing to admit that Jesus was a great moral teacher, but that's as far as they will go. He then cites numerous instances from Jesus's life where Jesus says things like "I forgive you your sins" and "Before Abraham was, I am." Lewis concludes that the only person who would say these things either was God or a complete lunatic, but certainly not just a great moral teacher.

At work, I was in the library when a fellow teacher walked up and began telling me about some things going on in her life, including a divorce, a mentally ill sister, and difficult roommates. She finished with, "I just don't know what to do anymore."

The next day I made a photocopy of those two pages from the book and handed it to her with a little explanation. As soon as I did it, it hit me. Oh my gosh—I am evangelizing. I'm becoming one of *those* people. I would never, ever have done this before Faith's birth.

In the middle of the week, Dr. Aragones reappeared. I greeted her with my usual "How is Faith doing?"

She gave me a polite smile and nod. "She is stable. Which is good."

I was very aware that she never mentioned the long line Dr. Bernard had vetoed, and I wasn't ever going to bring it up. I did have a question though.

I had been holding back on asking this, but since Dr. Aragones was leaving, I figured I might not get another chance. I was feeling more confident about Faith, but I wanted to hear it from the doctor. "Dr. Aragones, just what would you say Faith's chances are now?"

She smiled uncomfortably and looked to the side. "Well," she began. "She is about seventy percent there."

Her answer reinforced what I thought. Faith was still officially listed as "critical but stable" for a reason. She was still on a respirator; the reality was, healthy babies are not on respirators. They don't weigh 2 pounds. On the other hand, she was 70 percent there, which was very reassuring, especially coming from Dr. Aragones.

Dr. Aragones continued. "The key is to keep things stable and keep her growing. Keep her healthy and gaining strength." She folded her hands in front of her. "You know, Dr. Bernard has left and I am leaving soon also. But Dr. Syed and Dr. Hecht will be here more. You know there is going to be a new director?"

"Yes, I heard."

"Well, Dr. Hecht and Dr. Syed will help with the transition."

She was trying to reassure me. I reached out and took both her hands in mine. "Thank you so much for everything you've done for Faith."

She smiled and we gently embraced. I had once dreaded seeing Dr. Aragones. Now I would be missing her too. She had kept Faith alive, healthy, and moving forward. I felt we had been very blessed with such excellent doctors. And I had to wonder now, just who would be replacing her? And what would it mean for Faith?

The next morning I walked into the NICU upbeat and confident. Faith was 70 percent there. I found Gina standing next to the Isolette. Gina was a small, curly-haired nurse, always friendly and positive.

"Hi, Mr. Krech." She said it quietly. Very quietly.

"How are you?" I asked.

"Fine." She didn't look up when she spoke. Just sort of stared to the side. "Faith is good too," she added.

The whole room seemed quieter than usual. "Is everything okay?" I ventured.

Gina hesitated, finally looked up, then answered softly, "We lost a baby last night."

I felt the weight of the words right on my chest. "Oh," I said. "I'm sorry."

All she could manage was a nod. We stood silent for a few moments. Then I asked, "Had the baby been here long?"

"No," she said. She wiped her eyes. "He got here last night."

"I'm so sorry," I repeated.

She just nodded again and sniffed.

This was the first outright mention of a baby in the NICU dying. I knew it had to happen given the critical state of some of these infants, but it was sad and jarring to hear it firsthand.

Later that day we found Suzie on duty with Faith. Karen and I both bent our knees to get face-to-face with Faith in the Isolette. She was on her side. Her eyes open. She looked good. "How's Faith doing?" Karen asked.

"Very well. Our little darling is looking great," Suzie answered.

I straightened up and asked, "Have you heard anything about this new director yet?"

"Oh," she said casually. "He's right over there."

CHAPTER 30

Respirator

Just like with Faith's move to the incubator and her new shirt, it was just—*bam!*—here he is. I craned my neck to see around the columns of equipment. Karen said, "Oh? What's his name?"

"When did he start?" I asked.

"Dr. Richard Wilborn. This morning," she replied with a smile.

Standing next to an Isolette across the room was a tall, lanky guy with short brown hair and a close-cropped brown beard. He looked to be in his late thirties and was wearing a colorful Mickey Mouse scrub shirt. A small crowd of nurses surrounded him. He was shaking hands and laughing.

Karen asked, "Have you met him yet?"

"Yes. Earlier." She kept her eyes on him as she spoke. "He's from a very good hospital in Pittsburgh and has a great reputation. He has a wife and young son who are going to be joining him after he settles in."

I tried to catch his eye, but he was moving in the other direction and was soon out of sight. As we were getting ready to leave, however, another nurse came up to us. "Mr. and Mrs. Krech, Dr. Wilborn said that if I saw you, I should schedule a meeting. He wants to discuss an eye exam he's going to have done on Faith."

"Sounds good," I said. And we set up a time.

As we were leaving, Karen said, "He already knows who we are on his first day. That's probably a good sign."

"Yeah. I agree. Hard not to know though."

"And he scheduled the eye exam already."

"True."

It was a quiet Friday night when we had this meeting. Our first. Karen was home with Andrew. I was sitting alone near Faith's Isolette. Dr. Wilborn appeared and pulled up a stool, tucking his long legs underneath. We shook hands and as he glanced down into Faith's Isolette, he said admiringly, "You have quite a daughter."

He made it sound like Faith had just hit a couple of home runs. I smiled. "Yep. She's something."

He directed his attention to a manila folder. "Well," he said, "I'm sure you know some about ROP."

"Some, yes." From reading and talking with the nurses and doctors, we had learned that premature infants have a very high incidence of eye damage due to three factors: the degree of prematurity, the amount of time exposed to oxygen, and the percentage of oxygen encountered. Unfortunately, Faith had been born about as premature as you could get, she had been on oxygen over two months, and she had been exposed to large amounts. She had all three strikes against her.

Dr. Wilborn continued, "The eye disease preemies are most susceptible to is retinopathy of prematurity, or ROP. In ROP, too much oxygen causes hardening of the ventricles in the eyes. Depending on the severity, it could range from a need for glasses to blindness. I wanted to tell you about the eye exam. She's had some ROP, so there is some hardening of the ventricles, but it is not bad and it will most likely resolve itself."

I asked, "What does that mean long-term?"

Dr. Wilborn paused, then replied, "If she keeps going like this, there is a ninety percent chance she will have normal vision. She may have to wear glasses."

I felt the warm flow of relief wash over me once again. "Wow. That's great," I said.

He gave me a look. From his expression, I suspected he was thinking that I did not fully appreciate the incredible nature of Faith's eye condition. "It's pretty amazing," he said shaking his head. Then he added, "I wish I had your kind of luck."

I was uncomfortable with the idea of Faith's miraculous progress being reduced to a question of luck, and felt prompted to at least say something, so I smiled and said, "Well, there were a lot of prayers in there too."

He looked at me and said nothing. To fill the silence, I asked him a couple more questions about Faith's progress. He was conservative and careful in his answers, but I sensed a quiet confidence on his part.

Despite the excellent report from the ophthalmologist, it was now mid-January and Faith was still on constant oxygen support. We knew the health of her eyes and lungs remained at serious risk if she continued like this on the respirator.

The respirator was the classic double-edged sword. It kept her alive, but it would seriously harm her if she stayed on it. The breaths given by the machine expanded the lungs, but stiffened them through this action over time. The result was bronchopulmonary dysplasia, or BPD. We were fortunate all these medical conditions had acronyms because most of them were real mouthfuls.

Dr. Hecht had informed us that Faith already had BPD. She said it was inevitable given the amount of time Faith had been on the respirator. Fortunately, BPD is reversible in infants provided it is not too severe and the baby can eventually be weaned off the respirator.

A few moments after Dr. Wilborn left, Meera appeared at my side. As if she were reading my mind, she nodded toward the respirator. "Her rate is all the way down to ten. Her oxygen is in the mid-twenties. She is doing very, very good."

This was fantastic compared to where she'd started, but Faith had been down this low before and gone back up. I didn't say that out loud to Meera, but merely smiled appreciatively, nodded, and said, "That's really great to hear."

Meera spoke directly, her dark eyes fixed on me. "She is breathing so well, she doesn't need this tube anymore."

This was the first time anyone had said anything like that. I thought Faith would have to get down to a rate of zero to get off the respirator.

"Dr. Syed is coming on for the weekend shift," she said. "I think I am going to tell him she doesn't need the tube anymore. You should tell him too," she said.

I noticed she didn't say that I should tell Dr. Wilborn this. I guessed she probably felt she and I had more influence over Dr.

Syed at this point.

Twenty minutes later, Dr. Syed entered as if on cue. As he approached, Meera moved off to the side, but hovered within listening distance. I didn't want to be the pushy parent making medical recommendations to the doctors, but I didn't dare not ask, with Meera watching in the wings. After our usual Arabic greetings and a handshake, I brought the topic up with Dr. Syed. "It looks like Faith's at the lowest rate she's ever been. Do you think she might be getting off the respirator soon?"

Dr. Syed shrugged as he answered. "She is doing well, but I want to see her gain more weight and strength before she is taken off. Maybe in a week or two."

I nodded. "I see. Do you want her to get down to a certain level?" I asked.

He shook his head. "No. It is not a matter of just numbers. It's a combination of factors. Mostly, I do not want to take her off only to see her go right back on again."

"I understand," I said. It made total sense to me. I turned to see if Meera had observed me doing my duty, but she was gone.

The next day, Karen went in on her own for the Saturday morning visit while Andrew and I did some errands together. Karen found Meera standing next to Faith's Isolette. The first thing she noticed was that the white medical tape on Faith's face was missing. The tape that had been there to hold the respirator tube in place. If there was no tape holding the respirator tube, it meant––

Karen turned to Meera in astonishment. They began to cry and hug. "She knew she was ready," Meera bubbled.

Faith had what resembled a clear plastic cake-plate cover over her head. Karen had looked right past it. Meera explained, "This is an oxyhood. It allows oxygen to be available to her in a low percentage but without any pressure or breaths being done for her. She is breathing a mix that is just about room-air. All by herself."

Dr. Syed ambled over. He looked tired, but he was smiling. He must have worked through the night. He looked to Karen. "Mrs. Krech, I told Meera that if this does not work out and I have to thread another tube in Faith's nose, I am going to put one in her nose also."

They giggled together. It was another example of the doctor being open and willing to listen to the nurse's experience and intimacy with the baby. Only then did Karen notice the hand-printed sign on the Isolette. In big black letters it read, LOOK MOM AND DAD! I DID IT! NO MORE TUBE!

Karen didn't tell me the news when she came home that day. She kept it a surprise for my visit. When I got there in the afternoon and saw Faith, I welled up. She would not be on a respirator the rest of her life.

I walked over to the window so my tears wouldn't be as obvious. It was the window that overlooked the brick courtyard by the chapel. A light snow began to drift down gently from the gray sky. The wind whipped, tossing the tiny flakes up and down. The first snow of the season.

Here we all were, just as I had prayed we might be way back in November—all together in the warmth and light of the unit, in the snow, in the winter.

CHAPTER 31

Ripples

I bounded down the stairs to the chapel. Seeing Faith off the respirator had filled me with an incredible joy. I wanted to go and pray my thanks to God immediately and personally.

I leaned into the heavy wooden chapel doors, took a step in, and halted. Someone was sobbing. As my eyes adjusted to the dim, I saw two women in bulky winter coats and heavy boots kneeling together at the altar. It was baby Jamal's mother and grandmother. I had seen them in the NICU almost every day for the past month and a half. They were the only other family there as long as we were. We had exchanged hellos and some small talk, but I didn't really know them.

Bowing deep in prayer, their heads shaking slowly side to side, I could hear their choked whispers of "Jesus...Jesus...Jesus."

I stepped in and closed the doors gently behind me.

•••

With Faith in the hospital going on three months, friends would often ask me how I was doing. I heard a lot of "You must be so tired. You must be worn out going back and forth to the hospital every day."

When I said I was doing fine, I suspect people thought I was just putting on a brave front. It was the truth though. Faith was making incredible progress, and my part in all of it was nothing compared to the doctors and nurses. I just went home at the end of the visit and left everything in their hands. And God's. During those first three months at Mercer, I had seen quite a few babies pass through the NICU. Most stayed only a day or two. A smaller number remained for a week. Jamal was the only other baby I knew of that had been there about as long as Faith.

He was born very premature and unfortunately had many complications with his heart and lungs. I watched him have to go back and forth from the NICU to Children's Hospital of Philadelphia several times for surgery.

His mother was maybe seventeen. At her age, in her situation, it would have been so much easier to walk away from the whole scene and leave Jamal to someone else—her mother, a relative, an adoption—so she could start again. She was a child herself, but she stayed on, visiting almost every day.

The last I saw of Jamal, he was still in the NICU in his own tiny critical-care corner, still on a respirator after many, many months. Dangling above his Isolette was a sweet mobile of brightly colored plastic birds and clouds. A sign of hope and love despite it all. His mother and grandmother were right there by his side.

Now here they were in the chapel, kneeling, praying, and weeping for his recovery. Sincere, heartfelt, tearful prayers. Begging Jesus for healing. But it had been months and it had not happened.

I slid quietly into the very back pew and knelt to pray. A few minutes later they got up to leave. As they passed, we exchanged nods. The big doors closed heavily behind them.

I had to ask myself an uncomfortable question. Why was Faith doing so well, even getting off the respirator, while other babies, like Jamal, suffered through more pain and complications, or even passed away? Had prayers made a difference for Faith? I thought so. But then why not for Jamal?

Father O'Brien had told us that God always hears the prayer of a parent for a child. I didn't take much comfort from the idea that God would just hear my prayer and not do anything about it. When I got home that night, I looked to my new books for guidance with these questions.

In C. S. Lewis's *The Joyful Christian*, I found a chapter called "The Efficacy of Prayer." In it, Lewis boiled my problem with prayer down to two sentences: "For prayer is *request*. The essence of request, as distinct from compulsion, is that it may or may not be granted."

It was a simple statement full of wisdom. Just because a prayer was not answered in the way we asked, that didn't mean it wasn't heard, and it didn't mean it wasn't answered either. It's a very hard truth that the answer we get might not be the one we long for. It might be "yes," it might be "no," it might be "not yet." That sounds okay philosophically, but "no" is devastating to take when it is your child's life or suffering in question.

Christian author Chuck Colson echoed this sentiment about prayer in a radio interview that I heard later. He said, "Of course, this is not to say that religious believers automatically get miraculous recoveries whenever they pray. After all, prayer is not a magical incantation that puts God in our power. Prayer is communication with the living God, who responds to each of us individually."

I didn't like it, but it rang true to me because even Jesus prayed in this way. I remembered that much from church. We would hear the story every Good Friday. Matthew 26:39 describes how, alone in the Garden of Gethsemane––just before He is arrested, beaten, tortured, mocked, and executed—Jesus prays, "Father, if it is your will, take this cup away from me; nevertheless, not my will, but yours be done."

Jesus, the Son of God, the most holy, most righteous, most deserving person ever to walk the earth prays to be spared the horrible fate he knows lies ahead. He prays all through the night to the point where he is sweating blood. The result of His impassioned prayers? He is still beaten, tortured, crucified, and dies. Because it was the Father's will and ultimately for all our greater good.

But what a profound example of how to pray. To pray fully believing and knowing that God will hear our request, that it is in God's power to grant the request, but asking that His will, which is perfect for each of us, be done. Like Tony Evans had said, "Thy will, not my will." Like Jesus said, "Not my will, but yours be done."

I realized that with my limited human intelligence, I would never come to understand why God might allow Faith to live and others like Jamal to suffer or die. In Isaiah 55:9, God tells us, "As the heavens are higher than the earth, so are my ways higher than your ways, and my thoughts than your thoughts." His wisdom and will is not of our understanding. He has told us this much. I had to accept that, even if death might be part of His plan.

I'm sure to some this sounds like very convenient rationalization. If all goes well, God decided it was what you needed. If it goes badly, that was what was needed. You interpret events any way you like and God or prayer to God has nothing to do with it. It's just luck, plain and simple.

I couldn't accept that. It didn't resonate. It didn't have that ring of truth. In my heart I believed God had a plan. Holocaust survivor Vera Goodkin put it this way: "If you're willing to make a concession and say the limit of human understanding stops at a certain point, then you can salvage your faith." I chose to salvage my faith.

As I got into bed that evening, I carried the image of Jamal's mother and grandmother with me. Their hands clutching the altar as they prayed. Their sad, weary faces as they walked by me. I turned to Karen as she read next to me. "What do you think about our prayers and Faith?"

She set her book down on her lap. "What do you mean?"

"Do you think they make a difference?"

Karen paused, collecting her thoughts. She answered, "When Faith was born I was still struggling with Harold Kushner's ideas, and I didn't get a direct answer from Father O'Brien when I asked about God being in control."

I nodded. "I felt that too."

"But since we've been with Faith in the hospital," Karen continued, "I've seen that prayer does work. I know and accept that God is in control and He does things we just don't understand or allows things to happen that we never would, but that He's good and kind and I know Faith would not be here without Him."

I had moved along the same lines as Karen. I felt in my heart that our prayers and those of others made a difference in Faith's survival. I couldn't prove it, but I felt it. Because of my faith, I too finally had the courage to completely discard Kushner's easy, appealing, and logical answer, that God was not in total control, that He did what He could, but could not make everything come out well and right.

Instead I was working toward accepting what the Bible says—that even though there is horrible pain, heinous brutality and abuse, and unfathomable evil on earth, and we won't ever understand it all while we are here, God remains in control. Not only that, but that He will hear our prayers, be with us, and help us through it, even if coming through it means death and joining Him in eternity.

Much later, I would see a cartoon in the newspaper in which a cat is complaining to another cat, saying, "I was thinking of all my problems. I was thinking of all the pain of the past and I was thinking of all the uncertainty of the future." The other cat just listens, and the first cat goes on. "And I was thinking poor, poor me—my sad life. And then I was thinking how little time there is and I'm thinking it's all just...hopeless. What can I do?" The second cat stares and then says, "Stop thinking."

That's exactly what I would do before Faith's birth. When thoughts about my purpose in life, my relationship with God, the problem of pain and evil in the world would surface, I would simply stop thinking about it. It was a lot easier to turn those thoughts off and just move on. But Faith's birth had cut off my option of "not thinking" for good.

Faith was bringing Karen and me closer to God and closer to each other, but it wasn't just us she was changing. There was a real ripple effect going on.

It wasn't until almost five days after Faith was born when it suddenly dawned on me that I should get her listed on my health insurance coverage. In an absolute panic, I'd called my benefits representative at school, hoping it wasn't too late. Her name was Betty Royal.

At first, I knew her only as a cheery British voice over the phone, but I soon had a chance to meet her when I went to fill out the necessary forms. Betty reassured me and then took efficient care of the paperwork. Soon Karen and I were receiving shocking insurance statements in the mail every few days, detailing thousands of dollars of medical costs. By mid-January they totaled over $250,000. And we never had to worry about it because of Betty's work on our behalf. She also told me about Merwick House.

Merwick House was a branch of Princeton Medical Center in Princeton, New Jersey, specializing in convalescent care for the elderly. Betty's daughter was one of the directors at Merwick, and Betty was a regular volunteer. After Betty learned about our situation, she told me, "I've let the patients at Merwick know about Faith and almost all of them immediately began praying for her." Betty smiled broadly. "I was positively thrilled with this development."

"That's really nice," I replied.

"Oh, it's more than nice," she said. "These people badly need a focus outside of themselves, otherwise they tend to dwell completely on their own illnesses and pains. Faith helps provide them with a focus."

She continued, "Let me give you an example. During one of my evening tours of duty over there, I was going from room to room in the middle of the night, checking on everyone. I found one of our oldest residents sitting up in bed with her light on. She is a tough old bird. Very testy. Complains a lot. Everything has to be about her. Well, her TV was off, which was unusual, and she was not reading. She was just sitting up with her eyes closed."

I listened as Betty continued: "I thought, oh no, she's going to be on about something, just waiting to lay into me. But I figured, let's have it out. So I peeked in the room and asked quietly, 'Are you okay, dear?' With eyes still closed, she settled back into her pillow and replied, 'Yes, I'm fine.' I asked, 'Is there anything I can do for you then?' She said, 'No thank you.'"

Betty told me she'd persisted, asking, "What is it then? Can't you sleep?"

The old woman was quiet for a second, then replied, "I'm praying."

Betty said that she'd paused, then asked, "Oh? Is everything okay then?"

"Yes," the old woman had said. "I'm praying for Baby Faith."

CHAPTER 32

The Big Room

Saturday morning dawned bright and beautiful with good weight news greeting us at the NICU. It was written all in caps in bold black marker right next to the date on Faith's chart—January 23, 1993: 3 LBS! Three pounds and no respirator. It was a whole new era.

Karen playfully stroked Faith's miniscule foot. "You're getting so big. You are sooooo big!" Faith squirmed and kicked at Karen's fingers. I heard movement behind me and turned to see Pam wheeling an infant in an Isolette. We exchanged a wave, and they continued right on past us and into the transition room.

The NICU consisted of two large areas: the intensive care room where Faith was, and the transition room. We had never actually been in the transition room, only seen it through a bank of tinted windows in the adjoining wall. The nurses referred to it as the Big Room. It was exclusively for babies getting ready to transition out of the hospital.

The last two weeks of January were good ones for Faith. There were still A's and B's, and even though each time they occurred it essentially meant no breathing or a stopped heart, or both, the episodes were far less frequent, and shorter. Once when I was there during an episode, Red-Haired Debbie had said, "Hey, no big deal. She just forgot to breathe. You forget things too, Dad. And you see we took off the oxyhood. She just has this nasal cannula now."

I had seen cannulas before. Usually on elderly people. It was a plastic tube with two nodules positioned just under Faith's nostrils. A cannula seemed almost normal compared to all the other stuff.

Debbie had continued, "The tubing here leads to this oxygen tank. There's a dial that adjusts the amount released. It doesn't force it up her nose or do any breathing for her like the respirator, it just makes the oxygen available to her."

Seeing that big 3-pound weight on the chart was encouraging. So was just looking at Faith. She was rounder. Her movements smoother. She had a nice pink color. She was still tiny, but then again, she wasn't even supposed to have been born yet.

Pam came over and stood next to Karen and me. "You up for holding her?"

By now this was standard procedure, so I smiled and said, "Sure." I took a step back toward the rocker to sit down.

"Why don't you take her out," Pam replied. I halted. For emphasis, she flipped the top of the Isolette open and moved to the side.

"Uh, okay," I said. I had never paid attention before to how the nurses actually did this. Reaching into the small space of the Isolette was awkward. I had to bend at the shoulders and reach down and in. As I lifted, Faith's blanket fell off. I lowered her back. I wrapped the blanket more securely around her, tucking in both ends, and lifted again.

I got her about halfway up and was stopped short by heart monitor wires and an IV tube. I started to sweat. I had to put her down to free up my hands and move the wires and tube to the side. I glanced up at Pam, hoping she might have pity and take over. She gave me a small smile but didn't move an inch.

I tried again, making sure this time that everything was well separated. I wrapped the blanket tight and secured the ends; positioned my hands; lifted; got her up, over the edge, and out; walked three steps; and collapsed into the rocker.

Pam sauntered over, casually popped a cap on Faith's head, and said simply, "That was good."

"Thanks," I said breathlessly. Karen laughed. "Just wait," I said. "You're next."

To take some attention off of my ineptitude, I asked Pam a question. "I saw you bringing that new baby into the transition room before. Do you ever work in there?"

"Sometimes," she said. "A lot of us do."

Karen asked, "Is it easier?"

Pam gave a slight shrug. "It's just different. You get babies who have a problem stabilizing right after delivery, so they'll stay a night or two, mostly just for observation. Some stay longer as part of their overall treatment plan. It's a little more low-key."

It would be a big graduation day when it was decided Faith was well enough to make the move to the Big Room, but we were near the end of our third month and no one had mentioned it yet.

The following week we got more good news. Peg saw Karen that Monday, the first day of February. She was finishing up her shift, getting ready to leave. "Oh, guess what?" she said. "Tomorrow Faith is going to have a bottle."

She held up what looked like a plastic baby bottle from a child's doll set. Peg put the bottle in Karen's hand and said excitedly, "She was practicing nippling on this last night, and the way she's been eating, she looks ready."

"That's terrific," Karen said. "And it's just another 'normal' thing she can do."

"You bet," Peg said and gave her a wink.

The next night, we saw Peg with Faith again and she could hardly get the words out, she was so excited. "I gave Faith a bottle before and I can't believe she ate the whole thing! She ate the whole thing in one shot."

Apparently, Faith was very ready to eat like a big girl, and the nurses once again had known when it was time. Peg reported to us again the next day. "Okay. She calmed her eating down a bit. She took just a little of her feeding, but tolerated it well with no A's and B's. She needed more oxygen afterward, but other than that, she was fine. And she's up to three and a half pounds."

On Saturday morning, Karen and I were eating breakfast and making our plans for the day. I said, "I think I'll bring Andrew to the farmer's market with me." Lots of good food, delicious smells, and interesting action there with farmers and butchers and shoppers from all over the Trenton area. Andrew also always came away with a cookie from the Polish bakery, so he was game.

"That would be good. I'll go over to the hospital while you two are there."

Andrew and I headed out and Karen left right after. When she got to the unit, she marked her milk packets, FEB. 6, and put them in the freezer. Dr. Syed was there and greeted her.

Karen told him about our week. He shared the latest on Faith and then very casually said, "A little later today we are going to move Faith to the transition room."

The Big Room. Like out of nowhere. "Oh my gosh! That's great!" she said excitedly.

He looked over the yellow legal pad in his large hands. "Yes. There are just too many babies who require more care than Faith right now," he replied.

That was a statement Karen wasn't sure she would ever hear. She thanked Dr. Syed, went to Faith's Isolette, and sat down next to her. "It's a big day, Faith," she said. "You're going to move."

Peg stopped by and commented, "So, I hear we have a graduate. Moving on to bigger and better things."

Karen replied, "I think she heard Andrew was going to preschool, so she felt she needed to do something big too."

They both laughed and Peg said, "Congratulations. See you on the other side."

Half an hour later, a young nurse strolled in and without any introduction told Karen, "I'm going to move her."

Karen got up and helped pack Faith's diapers, shirts, tape player, and other belongings into the storage shelves in the bottom of the Isolette. The nurse silently unplugged the monitors and began wheeling the incubator across the room. Karen followed behind carrying the extra baggage.

Maybe she was new to the job, maybe she was in a hurry, maybe she had never had to wheel an Isolette before, but turning the first corner, the nurse rammed it right into a wall.

Karen stood stunned. She began to say something, but before she could, the nurse backed up, repositioned, and started again, moving quickly behind the nurses' station. Karen scrambled after her.

As the nurse turned the next corner, she rammed another wall, *hard*. The Isolette jolted to a stop, the storage doors flew open, and all Faith's gear poured out onto the floor.

The always-calm Dr. Syed exploded out of his chair, bellowing, "What is this?! What are you doing?!"

Karen and Dr. Syed checked to make sure Faith was okay while the nurse muttered an apology as she picked up Faith's things. Under the glower of the still-standing, red-faced neonatologist, the nurse slowly and carefully finished wheeling Faith into the Big Room. She quickly hooked up the Isolette and monitors and disappeared without another word.

Karen was upset that after all the special, careful care, Faith's big move turned out to be a wild ride that might have ended in an injury. But in the end, since Faith was fine, nothing could spoil the fact that she had arrived on the other side. I figured her next move could only be to one place—home.

But I was wrong. There was still one more move to make.

CHAPTER 33

Cribs

Later that afternoon I returned to the hospital with Karen. Walking from the intensive care room into the transition room, the lights were dimmer. It was quieter. Everything was more spread out. It was a different world.

Gina greeted us, tapping the incubator next to her and saying, "You've got a big girl here."

"Thank you," we said in unison.

Karen asked, "Are you assigned to her today?"

She shook her head. "It doesn't work like that in here. She won't have her own personal nurse like when she was a little princess in intensive care. She'll be one of three or four babies assigned to one person."

We laughed and Gina continued, "The goal now is to get her totally off any and all oxygen support." She nodded affirmatively as she added, "And she's getting there."

That's the way it stood through the next two days when on Monday, February 8, we walked in to find Faith's Isolette covered with a dozen homemade birthday cards and notes. Three months old. Another birthday her nurse pals marked for her. It didn't seem possible that so much time had passed.

Confirming Gina's prediction, the next morning I found

the nasal cannula lying in the bottom of the Isolette. Faith was breathing room-air with absolutely no assistance whatsoever, just like we were.

On Wednesday, however, during my morning visit, I noticed the cannula was back on. Suzie was standing nearby and I had to mention it.

She grinned and shrugged. "Oh, they always go on and off with that. Anyway, did you see her weight gain?" She pointed at the chart. "Look. Eighty grams."

I was shocked. "That's huge."

Suzie smiled broadly. "Yep. She's doing fine. Look at her."

I stroked Faith's head. So soft and warm. She did look very settled and calm.

Over the next few days, Faith went on and off the cannula. Karen asked Gina about it when we saw her that Friday night. "Well," she said, "it's not unusual for babies like Faith to go back and forth on the respirator several times before getting off for good."

I didn't realize her going back on the respirator was a possibility. I must have looked panicked because she quickly followed up with, "I'm not saying that's what's happening here. It does happen though. The cannula is very minimal assistance."

She said *cannula* again, but I kept hearing *respirator*.

On Saturday, February 13, Karen and I were there as Dr. Wilborn made his rounds. We stood by as he gave Faith a careful exam. Finally, he straightened up. He pulled a set of x-rays from a file. "Well, I've been checking into her oxygen needs and the x-rays look good," he said. "They show that the lung tissue is softening and the BPD is improving. The problem is that there's some fluid on the lungs."

"What could be causing that?" Karen asked. "How dangerous is this?"

"Her system just needs a little help," Dr. Wilborn assured us. "She's been having some large weight gains lately, and it looks like some of that could be fluid retention."

So Faith's recent wonderful weight gains were maybe a little too wonderful.

Dr. Wilborn continued, "I don't particularly like to prescribe diuretics for babies, but her system is not regulating itself well enough without them yet. So we'll give her a try on them until she can do it on her own. She's going to lose quite a bit of weight very suddenly, but don't worry."

•••

On Valentine's Day, Karen and I drove over for an evening visit. The clear plastic walls of Faith's Isolette were papered once again, this time with pink and red Valentine's cards. You could hardly see through the forest of cards to find Faith.

I glanced at her chart. "Karen," I said, "she lost three hundred grams! *In a day!*" I was shocked. The girl used to only weigh a total of 450 grams.

Karen responded patiently, "Dr. Wilborn said she would lose weight."

"I know, but three hundred grams?"

"We didn't know exactly how much to expect, and he did say

she was going to lose quite a bit. Anyway she's off the cannula."

It was true. She was breathing room-air again. Pam joined us. She had a preemie bundled in her arms. Some parents couldn't be around to hold their babies. Hospital volunteers, mostly older women, would take over in that department, holding and rocking babies throughout the day, but the nurses made time for it too. It was that important.

Pam pointed with her chin across the room. "Now we have to get her into a crib."

I looked around. "Where are the cribs?" I had never seen any cribs in the NICU. I still didn't.

"Right there." She nodded toward a row of contoured plastic buckets sitting on wheeled tubular metal frames. They were painted battleship gray and looked like dull, futuristic shopping carts.

"That's a crib?" I asked.

"Our version, yeah," she replied.

As unattractive as the NICU cribs were, that was where we hoped to see Faith next, and if a nurse like Pam casually mentioned something, it almost always meant that it was going to happen soon. "We'll move her into a crib when she can maintain her temperature out in the open air," she said.

Sure enough, the next evening, Karen and I arrived in the transition room to find that Faith's Isolette was not in its usual spot. As we wheeled around looking for her, a big Southern voice boomed, "Hey, y'all! Look who's in a crib."

Big Martha was on the other side of the room, motioning us

over. Big Martha was a large, friendly nurse originally from somewhere in the South. She had a kind, slow, easygoing manner.

We joined her across the room and there was Faith out in the
open air in a gray metal "crib." She was bundled and re-bundled
like never before.

Pam was there too. She said, "I put her in this morning. I
figured I'd give her a shot. She'll probably have to go back and
forth some between the Isolette and the crib till she gets the hang
of controlling her temp. That's typical."

Over the next few days, each time Karen and I turned the
corner into the transition room we would wonder where we would
find Faith—crib or Isolette? Each time, Faith had managed to stay
in the crib. She was controlling her temperature. Soon, nurses
were even leaving her cap off, though I usually popped it back on
her head before leaving. I also noticed that the cannula was most
often just lying in the crib, not under her nose.

•••

On Tuesday when we arrived, we were hailed by the ever-jolly
Red-Haired Debbie. When she spotted me she clapped her hands
and called across the room, "Oh goody, Mr. Krech. You're just in
time."

There was something about her tone. "Oh?" I replied warily.
"In time for what?"

I walked over to Faith's crib. The smell assaulted me.

Debbie took an exaggerated step back from the crib and
folded her arms. "That's right." She nodded. She dusted her hands
dramatically. "Your daughter's made a real mess in her diaper and

it's about time ol' Dad learned to change it. Ha, ha."

"Why do you always pick on me?" I asked. "Karen's right here too."

"'Cause I like you, Dad," Debbie replied. "You know that."

Karen laughed along with her. Attempting to rise to the occasion, I smiled back and said, "Okay. Sure."

Debbie pointed to a counter nearby. "Everything's laid out right over there. Changing pad, diaper, wipes, ointment. You know how to do this, right? You've already had one."

"Yes," I admitted.

"All right!" Debbie said enthusiastically. "She's all yours." She then immediately abandoned the room.

It was true that I had changed plenty of Andrew's diapers, but he had never been a tiny preemie sunk down in a curved plastic bucket. I rolled up my sleeves, plunged my arms in, scooped under her, and lifted carefully. I got her halfway up and was stopped short by heart monitor wires.

I was trying to work quickly and not expose Faith to the air for too long because I was concerned about her maintaining her temperature, but all my hurried fumbling prolonged the event and I ended up smearing Faith, her crib, and my shirt cuffs with her soft, brown, almost liquid mess.

Debbie returned after a few minutes, took one look, and shook with laughter. "Seriously, Dad? We better get you some more wipes."

Apparently, something in the food was not totally agreeing with Faith, or she enjoyed my distress with the first diaper change, because as soon as diaper changing was added to our duties, it seemed to me that she started having much larger, looser, and more frequent bowel movements.

Near the end of the week, Peg taught Karen and me how to draw Faith's medications up into a syringe and add them in proper dosages to her bottle. We were being trained to handle a lot more of Faith's care. This clearly pointed to an exciting possibility—discharge.

•••

Andrew pressed his hands and face to the glass as if he would like to climb in. Rows of shiny chip bags and colorful jumbo candy bars filled the brightly lit vending machine. At two, he still found it a joyous miracle that you could get potato chips from a machine. Every time we took him with us to the NICU, the first thing he would ask was, "Can we go to the Machine?"

It was Thursday, February 18. After indulging in a bag of chips and a quick hand wash, we were off to the sibling playroom.

Karen went in to see Faith first while I stayed with Andrew. When she walked into the transition room, she was greeted by the loud crying of an unhappy baby. It was not unusual to hear babies crying in there, but as Karen walked across the room, she realized it was coming from Faith's crib.

We had heard a few small grunts and gasps from Faith before, but this was a full-throated yell. It had taken a long time for her esophagus to heal after having had the tube running down it for so long. But, boy, when she healed, she demonstrated her vocal power.

Karen scooped Faith up out of the bucket and held her tight to her chest. "Wow, sweetie," she said. "You have a big voice."

Faith was not impressed by the attention. She just wanted something to eat, and now. When my turn came, I brought Andrew in with me. Faith was still crying. Andrew clapped his hands over his ears. "She's loud," he said.

"You got a noisy kid there," Pam remarked.

"I guess so," I said. Faith's crying and all of our recent preemie-care training prompted me to ask Pam, "So, what is considered an acceptable discharge weight?"

She smiled, arching an eyebrow at me, and said, "They're usually around five pounds."

I glanced down at Faith's chart: 4 pounds and 7 ounces.

CHAPTER 34

Leaving

K aren had just come into the kitchen from grocery shopping with Andrew. As she put the bags down on the table,
Andrew began to imitate a jet plane and flew off into the
family room. The phone rang. It was Tuesday, March 2. A woman's
friendly voice on the other end announced, "This is the director
of public relations at Mercer Medical Center. How are you doing,
Mrs. Krech?"

Karen replied, "Good. Thank you" while at the same time
wondering why public relations would be calling her.

"Well, I'm phoning on behalf of the hospital. We were hoping
that you and Faith might be willing to be part of our new publicity
campaign highlighting the NICU. We're going to do some print
ads, a radio spot, and a television commercial for local stations.
Do you think you could participate with us?"

Karen heard that and she knew right then that Faith had made
it. If the hospital was going to advertise Faith's story, the professionals must finally believe she was going to be all right. So maybe
we should too.

That night I called Father O'Brien. I hadn't seen or spoken to
him since our first meeting all those months ago. His secretary
answered, saying, "He's not in right now. Can I take a message?"

I said, "Yes. Would you tell him that Faith Krech, the preemie baby at Mercer..." I couldn't believe I was going to say it out loud. "Could you tell him that she's going to be all right?"

From that point the last reluctant pieces of Faith's development fell rapidly into place. Developmentally, she was now on schedule to be born, and you could see it.

She was taken off the diuretic. She was gaining normal weight, not water weight, in regular daily upticks. She was breathing without any oxygen assistance. She was holding her temperature without intervention. She was getting Karen's breast milk in a bottle, along with vitamins and medications, and even beginning to learn to breastfeed.

All of this progress prompted the ever-vigilant Aunt Meera to begin a new campaign. With perfect timing, the day after the publicity department called, Meera sidled over to Karen and me. "Faith is ready, you know. It is time for her to be released."

"Oh. Really?" Karen replied.

"You think so?" I asked.

"Yes. If we keep her longer, we might expose her to something unnecessarily. We don't want that. You need to tell Dr. Wilborn," she insisted.

There was no resistance possible on my part when it came to Meera's "suggestions." In a scene very reminiscent of my discussion with Dr. Syed about Faith's getting off the respirator, I approached Dr. Wilborn that evening while Meera waited nearby to ensure I followed through.

I meandered into the question. "So, Dr. Wilborn, what's your thinking on Faith going home?"

He answered, "We'll keep her on till we're sure she won't need any oxygen support at home and her medications are down to a minimum."

I nodded and said, "I see."

My face must have shown some disappointment, though, because he quickly reassured me, "Bob, we want you and Karen to go home and be parents, not medical technicians."

That was a good way to put it. And to be honest, there was a good part of me that was in no desperate hurry to get Faith home. That might sound strange after having her in a hospital for four months, but we knew she was getting the best care possible right where she was, and I was more than a little bit nervous about how Karen and I would do on our own with such a tiny infant.

The next day, though, I went up into the attic and brought down Andrew's crib. I cleaned it up and reassembled it in the bedroom that would be Faith's. I carried the cradle up from the basement and into our room next to the bed. It was getting real.

Dr. Wilborn asked to meet with us again Saturday, March 6, Faith's actual, original due date. How appropriate that he ended his report with "Things have moved along really well for her this week. So...I'm scheduling discharge for next Sunday, the fourteenth."

Karen and I took turns shaking Dr. Wilborn's hand and hugging him. After all those weeks and months, there was now an end date in sight.

Faith had her vision and hearing checked on Monday. Dr. Jason Lowenthal, a pediatric eye specialist, did an exam that indicated

Faith's ROP was still resolving. It was satisfactory enough for discharge without eye surgery of any sort being necessary. I finally went out and bought the second car seat.

•••

We left the house that Wednesday evening, March 10, heading to the hospital and feeling confident and energized. It was good news every day now. Good breathing. Good feeding. Good weight gains. Spring was coming too. You could feel it in the soft warming of the air. We saw Pam as we entered. "I hear you've got an exit date, huh?"

"Yep," I replied. "Sunday."

"You two ready for this?" she asked wryly.

Karen smiled. "I guess we'd better be."

"Aw, you'll do fine." Pam walked over to Faith and looked down at her. She shook her head. "That kid's come a long way."

Yep, I thought. Thank God for that. We sat down next to Faith's crib. She was swiveling her head around, gazing up in all different directions. "She looks busy," Karen remarked.

"Yeah," I agreed. "So much to see. She's got to take it all in before she leaves."

As Karen and I sat there, Liz, a trim, athletic-looking veteran nurse, walked by, gave us a smile, then stopped. She bent over, looking closely at the monitor near the crib. She made a small "hmmm," then picked the cannula up from Faith's blanket and slipped it back under her nose. My radar went up. "How's she doing there?" I asked.

"Her oxygen was a little low," Liz answered.

As we sat and watched Faith, within the hour Liz stopped back two more times, turning the oxygen higher each time. Suddenly, it looked like Faith needed a constant flow of oxygen. Karen and I usually left for home after an hour, but we were glued to our chairs.

Liz flagged Dr. Syed down as he moved among the babies on his rounds. "Doctor? Could you look at Faith, please? She hasn't been oxygenating well."

Karen and I pulled our chairs back to make room. Dr. Syed bent over Faith and moved his stethoscope around her chest. I searched his face for clues. He didn't say anything but left the room, returning a few minutes later with Dr. Wilborn. I was trying hard not to panic.

They checked Faith over together and talked in low voices between themselves as they flipped through her chart. It looked to me like all this attention and poking around was stressing her. I could see her SAT numbers on the monitor dipping further.

The doctors spoke to Liz and walked, heads together, back to the office. Liz gathered Faith's equipment into the bottom of her cart. "They want to bring her next door for x-rays. Be right back."

Liz wheeled Faith to the intensive care side. Karen and I stood there next to the empty spot where the crib had been. We didn't say anything aloud, but I knew we were both thinking something bad had just happened very suddenly. I began to pray in earnest, *Please let her be okay.* We had come so far.

Ten minutes later, Liz wheeled Faith back in. Then both doctors rejoined us. Dr. Wilborn said, "A quick read shows her lungs look fine."

This was a relief, but I still had to ask. "What do you think is going on then?"

Dr. Wilborn shrugged slightly. "It could just be stress. Or fluid again. We'll have to check a few things."

I groaned inwardly. Faith was so close to being out. Dr. Wilborn said, "I think we'll do a brain scan just to be on the safe side."

I was now officially 100 hundred percent frightened.

As Dr. Wilborn made some notes, Liz leaned over the crib and gently turned Faith's head from side to side. She straightened up and walked over to a cupboard. "I'm going to check something," she said. She reached in and brought out a small bottle of saline solution and a rubber squeeze bulb.

We all stood and watched as she held Faith's head with one hand and sprayed the saline solution up each nostril. Faith flinched with each squeeze. Liz repeated the spraying routine once more, then moved the squeeze bulb up into the first nostril. She squeezed, released, then pulled the bulb back. She moved to the next nostril. She squeezed and this time slowly drew the bulb out. At the tip hung a huge, dark, rock-hard booger (as my second graders would describe it).

Faith's SAT numbers rebounded immediately. She was breathing normally again. Liz handed the long blue squeeze bulb to Karen. "Here, you're going to need this at home," she said with a smile. The doctors and the rest of us looked on nonplussed. Faith's final emergency was behind her.

•••

Our visits during the final few days were focused almost

exclusively on "taking care of preemie babies at home" training. Each time, the nurses made us practice infant CPR with a plastic preemie doll. I was praying I would never, ever have to use infant CPR, but I would know how if I had to. Peg gave us two infant CPR posters with step-by-step instructions and cartoon illustrations. I took them home and taped the big one on the back of Faith's bedroom door and the smaller one on the side of the refrigerator. Not our usual décor, but this was not our usual life anymore.

The nurses coached us in measuring and administering medications, bathing Faith, and using a heart monitor. Red-Haired Debbie continued to put me on the spot. "Faith's going to be on this heart monitor until the doctors decide it's totally safe to remove her final wires, right? So let's see you hook this gizmo up."

We had practiced this. I picked it up off the counter, put the stickers on Faith's chest, connected the wires, and turned on the machine. It beeped to indicate it was hooked up properly and ready. Debbie nodded approvingly. "Not too shabby, Pops. I think you'll do fine."

"I'd better," I replied. Because according to the schedule, tomorrow would be Faith's final full day in the NICU.

But then, few things with Faith had ever gone according to schedule. And the next day would prove to be no exception.

CHAPTER 35

State of Emergency

It was still dark as I rolled out of bed at 6:00 a.m. I was figuring that I would do an early hospital visit before coming home and helping to get everything ready for Faith's homecoming. I glanced out the window into the backyard and the ground looked very white, maybe from the moonlight. As I got a better look, I saw it was snow.

I must have missed the weather report or maybe they'd gotten it wrong again, because this was a complete surprise to me. It looked like just a dusting, though, and it was only lightly flurrying. I bundled up, pulled on some boots, and guided our car down the street toward Trenton.

At the hospital, all was good. Faith looked terrific and had good numbers too. After about twenty minutes, I got up and walked out of the Big Room over to the window overlooking the chapel courtyard to check the weather.

The steps to the main entrance and all the bushes were blanketed with snow. It looked like another inch had fallen since I had left the house, and that was less than an hour before. I went back in, hastily said goodbye to Faith and the nurses, and headed home.

The usual fifteen-minute ride back took forty-five minutes, with cars all around me slipping, sliding, and spinning their wheels as the snow and wind picked up.

I got the car up our little hill of a driveway and into the garage on the third try in low gear. I took off my boots and quickstepped up the stairs into the laundry room. Karen called out to me, "Did you hear this?"

I hung my coat up and headed into the kitchen. She had the radio on loud: "We are expecting from ten to fourteen inches of snow in central and northern New Jersey. Governor Florio has declared a state of emergency. All nonessential vehicles are ordered off the roadways by nine o'clock."

"How was the hospital with this storm?" Karen asked.

"Everything looked fine. We could call and check though," I offered.

Karen immediately picked up the phone and called the NICU. Gina answered. "How are things going over there?" Karen asked.

Gina calmly reassured her, saying, "We've got it all covered, Mrs. Krech. Everyone on duty is just staying. The next shift was told not to come in. We have two doctors here and we have an emergency backup generator in case the city loses power so please don't worry."

As the snow continued to fall throughout the day, we called twice more to check in. Meera answered the second call in the evening. She sounded cheerful. She probably enjoyed an emergency like this. "We are doing back-to-back shifts," she informed us. "We have rooms to sleep in too. No problem. Faith is fine. We are all fine."

It snowed hard through the night, finally petering out early

Sunday morning. As we looked out the front door at the sea of sparkling white, Karen asked, "Do you think we'll be bringing her home today? Or tonight?"

I couldn't tell where the street ended and our lawn began. There was probably about three feet of snow. "I don't know about that," I replied.

Karen called the hospital and got Gina once again. "Do you think we will be able to take her home today?" Karen asked anxiously. "She was scheduled for discharge, but with the snow..."

"Hold on. I'll check," Gina answered.

She came back with the word a few minutes later. "I'm sorry. We'll have to keep her another day. But if you can make it in later, you can spend the night with her here if you like."

Karen was excited by the offer and eager to do it. "Yes! Definitely," she said.

Fortunately, Sunday was sunny and warm. We spent most of the day shoveling out as the snow melted, with breaks to help Andrew build a snow fort and a snowman. Plows came rumbling by twice, opening up our street to the rest of the world.

Around 4:00 p.m., we dropped Andrew off at Grandma and Grandpa's and made our way back to Mercer. Gina greeted Karen warmly in the NICU. Then she reached into the crib, picked Faith up, and placed her in Karen's arms. "Follow me, Kreches," she said. "All three of you." She led us through the scrub room and then opened the door into the hall. "After you," she said politely.

It felt surreal that we were allowed to walk out of the NICU with Faith. It was the first time since her birth that she had been beyond those walls. We followed Gina down the hallway to a beautiful maternity room. It had wood furniture, drapes, wallpaper, and all the homey touches.

"This is nice, right?" Gina asked.

Karen nuzzled Faith. "What do you think, Faith?"

"This is nice," I said. "You might have trouble convincing them to go home."

Gina laughed. "No. I think they're pretty ready." She hooked up the heart monitor to the wall and connected it to Faith's sticky chest tabs.

"So, what time should I come tomorrow?" I asked.

"Give us a call in the morning to be sure, but I think it will be around nine," she replied.

I hung out for a while, then kissed Karen and Faith good night and headed home.

That night, alone with our baby for the first time, Karen attempted to clip Faith's fingernails before bed. These were extremely tiny fingers with almost invisible fingernails. It was no easy task, and she accidentally clipped Faith's finger. It began to bleed and Karen had to ring for a nurse and explain the situation.

A few minutes later, she heard a knock on the door. She looked up to find the doorframe filled by the presence of Big Martha holding up a Band-Aid and a tube of first-aid cream. "Need these?" she asked.

After the Band-Aid was on, Karen and Martha sat talking together. Other nurses took turns visiting during the evening, reminiscing and saying their goodbyes. After four months, Faith was leaving the only home she had ever known. Karen figured she would make sure Faith slept well, so at about 10:00 p.m. she said, "You want to eat, Faith? A little something before bed?" She started breastfeeding. Faith finally decided she was done at about 1:00 a.m.

Monday morning, I called to confirm that everything was still on schedule. Dr. Hecht got on the phone. Very casually she said, "Hi, Bob. You want to come and get your baby?"

I laughed and answered, "Sure. Why not?"

"Very good. Come in about eleven. I think we've got a couple of late sleepers on our hands."

"Well, I know that's Karen. Maybe Faith is just like her mom."

"Pretty sure that's true. I'll be doing the discharge with you guys. Dr. Wilborn is stuck in Pittsburgh. The airport there is still closed from the snow."

So Faith's old friend, Dr. Hecht, the doctor who had been there to check her in, was now going to check her out.

Andrew and I drove in and parked in the same lot I'd been parking in all winter. But this time when I got out of the car, it was with an indescribable lightness. It was real. She was going home!

Karen's sister Debbie joined us at the hospital. She immediately began filming everything. We met Karen and Faith in their lovely room. We hugged and packed up together. Suzie appeared at the door and asked, "Ready to check out, guys?"

"Oh yeah," Karen said, beaming. "Right, Faith?" Faith looked up into her eyes. No noise. No moving around. Just soft and still and quiet.

"She can't talk yet," Andrew informed Suzie.

"Oh, that's right. I forgot," Suzie quipped.

We trailed behind Suzie back into the NICU. We were greeted by an explosion of cheers and clapping. It looked like every NICU nurse we had ever met was gathered there. A colorful banner hung at the entrance. Splashed across it, glitter letters spelled out CONGRATULATIONS, FAITH!

A table was covered with cards and food. Instead of handing us a diploma, Dr. Hecht gave us a hug, a stack of discharge paperwork, a heart monitor, a plastic bag filled with preemie diapers, Faith's one medication, liquid vitamins, and two long blue rubber squeeze bulbs with bottles of saline solution.

I looked over the papers. Faith's final weigh-in at the hospital was 5 pounds, 4 ounces. She would be going home on a simple heart monitor and one medication. That was all for a baby who had been born at less than a pound and only twenty-two weeks old.

I felt blessed, proud, excited, and scared all at once. And also a tinge sad. This was a celebration, but it was also a parting from people we had come to know and love—people we had depended on every second of every day for four months. People who had saved our daughter's life.

A big sheet cake was wheeled in. Cameras flashed as nurses called out congratulations. As the cake was sliced and served, I found myself next to Gina. I wasn't sure if or when I would see any of these folks again, and I wanted them to understand how thankful I was. I said to Gina, "I hope you know how much Karen and I appreciate what you all did. I mean, we know you saved her life."

Gina wiped tears from her eyes with one hand while balancing her cake and fork in the other. She shook her head and said, "You know, you guys are the reason she did so well. You were always here, talking to her, holding her, touching her. All these things make a difference. We know it from the research, and we know it from experience. They need their parents' love and touch, and you always gave that to her."

Now it was my turn to balance cake and wipe tears. One of my constant prayers while Faith was in the hospital was that God would use her nurses and doctors—that He would give them the wisdom, know-how, and strength to care for Faith so she would survive.

Faith had five different neonatologists directing her case at different stages. Each time there was a change in doctor, I secretly feared that switching and the varied opinions and styles would result in conflict and confusion, and care that was uneven or contradictory.

Looking back, though, it seemed that each doctor contributed a special idea or treatment at just the right moment. Each was the right person at the right time. And I believe God's hand was in that.

But Gina made clear to me that God had used Karen and me as well. We all—nurses, doctors, therapists, and friends—we all were part. "I am the vine. You are the branches," Jesus said. Faith's survival emphasized the fact to me that God does most of His work, even most of His miracles these days, not through incredible, supernatural phenomena like burning bushes or parting seas, but through His people and their everyday actions, big and small.

We are the body of Christ. I'd heard that plenty of times at church. I used to think that just meant that we were a body of people, like a group or congregation. But I came to understand that we are also His physical body here on earth. We are His arms and legs to go to people who need help. His voice to tell everyone about the Word of God, and His eyes to see the needs that should be filled. With Faith, He had used the doctors, the nurses, and two scared parents to perform His miracle.

He had even used Faith to perform another, different kind of miracle. Because of her, God had become a daily reality in my life. Up to Faith's birth, nothing had changed my casual relationship with God, the neat little pocket of time and money I had assigned Him. Not even saving me from sure death in a car accident. Apparently, I was not alone in this. I later found a quote from C. S. Lewis about losing his wife to cancer. He wrote, "Nothing will shake a man, or at any rate a man like me....He has to be knocked silly before he comes to his senses."

Only Faith had knocked me silly. God used her to finally bring me closer to Him in a very real way. There is a contemporary Christian song by Laura Story called "Blessings." In it is the line, "What if trials of this life are Your mercies in disguise."

I would never have wished for Faith to have been born this way and to go through all we did. I would have preferred to remain comfortable, but without that trial, I would never have been changed the way I was.

After a stream of goodbyes, we made our way to the elevator and down to the front entrance. Andrew was holding my hand and skipping alongside us. Karen was being pushed in a wheelchair with Faith cradled securely in her arms. We used Andrew's old infant snowsuit for her first foray into the world outside. It was powder blue with huge piles of furry white trim. Once inside it, she was bundled till all that could be seen were two bright blue eyes.

We still didn't know exactly what we were about to face with Faith. Would she be frail? Would she have physical disabilities? Cognitive disabilities? I prayed she would be okay in every possible way, but for now she was alive, she was healthy, and she was coming home. And that was far, far more than any of us ever thought possible.

I stepped out the front door and sprinted across the parking lot. My heart pounded as I hopped behind the wheel and started the engine. I pulled up to the front entrance. For the first time, there were two car seats in the back of our silver minivan.

Karen and I carefully loaded and strapped Faith and Andrew in the back and slid the doors closed. We looked like a typical middle-class suburban family going for a drive somewhere on a sunny, cold Monday morning in March.

I honked the horn as we pulled away. Karen and Andrew waved to the security guards and nurses huddled by the front door against the wind. I drove the same route up Bellevue Avenue that we had driven with Andrew two and a half years before and had repeated so many times over the past winter. Our families were gathered at our house waiting to welcome Faith.

I turned right at the light and pointed the car toward home.

EPILOGUE

Going into the final five minutes, the soccer game was tied 1–1. Late-afternoon shadows cut across the bright green grass of the field. It was the last game of the 2003 fall season for the Lawrence Comets. At eleven and twelve years old, the girls could really play now. It wasn't like when they were six and chasing butterflies during the game.

The opposing team had the ball and were charging hard toward the Comets' goal. Suddenly, a tall forward blasted a shot unchallenged, the ball soaring high and hard toward the upper right-hand corner of the net.

The Comets' goalie leaped, a blur of red and white, stretching every inch of her frame. Her fingertips touched the ball just as its path took it directly above her head. It halted and spun for a second in midair, then deflected out of its trajectory to the ground. She pounced on it. The crowd roared.

The goalie quickly scooped up the ball, strode a few paces, and expertly booted it downfield. Spirits ignited by the spectacular save, the Comets took possession and two minutes later they scored again to secure the win.

At the final whistle, the goalie ran out to midfield, arms thrust in the air. The rest of the Comets encircled her, cheering and hugging. All the other girls were at least a head taller and a year older than she was.

Why did the smallest and youngest kid on the team choose to play goalie? It might have something to do with her competitive nature, her feistiness, the opportunity to use her quickness and reflexes. I'm not sure at all why she chose to be at the center of things—pitcher in softball, point guard in basketball, goalie in soccer. You'd have to ask Faith.

A few months after her discharge, we took Faith for a follow-up exam with Dr. Lowenthal, the pediatric eye specialist who'd first seen her at Mercer. It was a painful thing to watch and I'm sure to feel. He had to use some kind of metal instruments to keep her eyes pried open for the exam. She cried and screamed through the whole thing.

After it was over, Karen held Faith tenderly, kissing her gently and calming her down. We sat in the examining room as Dr. Lowenthal shared his findings. "This is amazing," he said. "Her ROP is *completely* resolved. Her vision is normal. She may need glasses sometime in the future, but that's about it."

"That's great," I said.

Dr. Lowenthal studied me. It was the same look Dr. Wilborn had given me when discussing the ROP. I could tell he felt I was underwhelmed by the news. "You have no idea how great this is," he said. "Do you know what the statistics are with something like this? With this degree of prematurity and the amount of oxygen?"

I mumbled about how it was indeed amazing.

He continued, "But you know the nurses at Mercer are very good. They are excellent with ventilator regulation, and that can make all the difference with this."

"They're excellent with everything," I said.

Faith's hearing was normal as well. She has never gone back

to the hospital except for preemie reunions with her doctor and nurse friends. In elementary school she never missed being on the honor roll. She had some perceptual lags and attended a special early-intervention preschool, but was placed in a regular kindergarten after that. She is highly skilled at "compensating," as the learning specialists like to say.

She was voted Peacemaker of the Year by her elementary school peers and was selected for her league all-star teams in both soccer and softball while playing on a travel basketball team. She is an aggressive player and learner. She certainly retains the fighting spirit the nurses described from her first hours on earth. I'm starting to let myself believe that she's going to be fine. I've even considered taking the infant CPR poster off the side of the fridge now that she's graduated college and working.

Karen went on to raise our kids while teaching elementary school and now works as a volunteer teacher in ESL for adults. Andrew is an award-winning photojournalist and social media manager at Elon University. Faith graduated from Guilford College in Greensboro, North Carolina, and works creating, writing, and editing websites. Andrew, who graduated from college right down the road at very preppy Elon, describes Guilford as a granola-eating, sandal-wearing, peace-and-justice, hippie kind of school. Faith would happily agree.

She was an honors student majoring in English and religious studies, involved in the Quaker traditions there. She traveled on a service trip with the school to Palestine and Israel. She volunteered at a Quaker convalescent home each week, spending a lot of time talking with the residents and interviewing them as part of her interest in journalism. Her sports are now Ultimate Frisbee and hiking.

As Andrew said, it's a hippie school.

As for Karen and me, we agree that by entering our lives when she did, as she did, Faith changed us both forever. We both start every day now with our Bibles and prayer. As our kids grew, we read a devotional with them every night. I feel like I'm in constant conversation with God through prayer.

I think back often to that moment when Faith was almost lost and we had nothing left in our own power that we could do or control. I had prayed and cried and worried and then those verses came drifting out of nowhere, and I thank the Holy Spirit for dropping them in on me, because that's what I believe happened. Now that I study the Bible regularly, read commentaries, and belong to a small group, I've come to understand the context of those verses better.

In Matthew 7:7–11 (New Living Translation), Jesus says, "Keep on asking, and you will receive what you ask for. Keep on seeking, and you will find. Keep on knocking, and the door will be opened to you. For everyone who asks, receives. Everyone who seeks, finds. And to everyone who knocks, the door will be opened."

Jesus was talking about seeking the kingdom of God and about asking for things that would support that like patience, wisdom, and guidance. He was not saying, "I'm your genie. Tell me whatever you wish for and I will grant it." At that moment though, I just took it as ask for whatever it is you want and be persistent. I wasn't really seeking the kingdom of God, I was just asking for a miracle for myself.

The Bible is a living document though. When we read and pray about the Word, we interact with God through the work of the Holy Spirit. I believe I was led to this verse for both purposes: to seek Faith's survival and to seek God. Both came together for me. God is pretty amazing that way, I've come to find.

My other verse, Matthew 17:20, where Jesus scolds His disciples for not having enough faith to drive a demon out of a young boy, is a similar example. Jesus says, "You don't have enough faith. I tell you the truth, if you had faith even as small as a mustard seed, you could say to this mountain, 'Move from here to there,' and it would move. Nothing would be impossible."

Again, I took it then to mean that if I just had a little faith, God could do the impossible for me. That it would be done, if it was in His will. Jesus wasn't saying that a mountain would literally move, but that the mountains in our lives, things that seem impossible to overcome, like saving Faith, are possible with God.

At the same time, I have to work at it every day to keep God at the center of my life and trust Him. I still pray those same words almost daily: "I believe, help me with my unbelief." But as journalist Julia Baird wrote in a *New York Times* op-ed piece, "Just as courage is persisting in the face of fear, so faith is persisting in the presence of doubt."

I thank God that He gave me a little faith, and then went on and showed me what great things even a little faith can do.

AFTERWORD

A sea of glistening paved road stretched out before my dad and me as we finished up our three-mile morning run in the stifling South Carolina heat. Rounding the final corner onto my parents' street, we slowed down and ran smack into a neighbor buzzing around her manicured bushes.

Springing toward me, the wiry woman with an emphatic grin reached out her gloved hand. "So, you're the miracle baby!"

Sweat poured down my face as Eminem's "Lose Yourself" abruptly halted, my finger jamming the pause button. I should be used to this greeting by now. I should have an arsenal of prepackaged lines loaded and ready, but hearing the word *miracle* attached to me is deeply humbling and always leaves me speechless.

This September, I returned to the story of my miracle birth through my father's manuscript, *A Little Faith*. Reading it exposed me to many scenes from those early years I had never heard about before. As I read, I found myself returning to the same question: "If I had been in my parents' shoes, how would I have reacted?"

The story challenged me to reflect on my life and spiritual pathway. Grasping the stark medical prediction of certain death or disability, followed by the fact they permitted me the chance to fight, was and is a precious gift. I think it's a gift that comes with a responsibility to make a positive impact. A charge to leave this earth a better place.

I am so blessed and privileged to stand without a walker or breathe without an oxygen tank. I feel it's the least I can do when countless others are not as lucky as I am. This newfound energy could manifest itself in a simple smile to a stranger or be a catalyst for something like committing a year of my life to aiding an underserved population.

Spiritually, this story threw me for a loop. Post-college I have wrestled with the existence of God. Possibly a symptom of craving to break away from the conservative boundaries between what I desired and what I thought was morally acceptable. Reading my story, I was reminded of my own core belief systems that had been buried for quite some time.

I believe in spirituality, the connection from one human to another that we all share. I believe that with this intimate thread binding us together we have a responsibility to love and protect each other. Reading about the interactions between the doctors, nurses, and my parents strengthened this belief.

After putting down the final page of the manuscript, I was left with an immense feeling of gratitude and pride toward my parents. I was astounded that even expert opinions couldn't shake their faith and conviction that I would live. Without their unwavering love and support, I certainly would not be here. I want to take this opportunity to express my gratitude and let them know how eternally grateful I am to them for believing in me always and, against all odds, never giving up on me.

Thank you, and I love you.

Faith Krech
Raleigh, North Carolina
November 2019

SELECTED RESOURCES

The Case for Christ: A Journalist's Personal Investigation of the Evidence for Jesus by Lee Strobel (Zondervan, 1998) Retracing his own spiritual journey from atheism to faith, Strobel, former legal editor of the *Chicago Tribune*, cross-examines a dozen experts, challenging them in a quest for the truth about history's most compelling figure.

The Case for Faith: A Journalist Investigates the Toughest Objections to Christianity by Lee Strobel (Zondervan, 2000) Legally trained investigative reporter Lee Strobel examines the claims of Jesus Christ through intensive interviews with experts.

Draw the Circle: The 40 Day Prayer Challenge by Mark Batterson (Zondervan, 2012) God honors bold prayer and bold prayer honors God. Batterson takes us through forty short, but powerful chapters written around this theme.

The Joyful Christian: 127 Readings by C. S. Lewis (Macmillan, 1977) This book includes many of Lewis's best essays, including two personal favorites, "What Are We to Make of Jesus Christ?" and "The Efficacy of Prayer."

Miracles: What They Are, Why They Happen, And How They Can Change Your Life by Eric Metaxas (Dutton, 2014) Inspiring, scholarly, and personal. Metaxas explores and explains the biblical thinking on miracles as well his own personal experience and that of others today.

The Purpose Driven Life: What on Earth Am I Here For? by Rick Warren (Zondervan, 2002) Clear, powerful guide that challenges you to really live as a Christian.

Time with God: The New Testament for Busy People (Word Publishing, 1991) Parcels the New Testament into 365 readings, each matched with a related Old Testament scripture and short commentary by a variety of notable Christian writers, including Tony Evans, Andrew Murrary, Max Lucado, and others.

The Urban Alternative A daily radio broadcast featuring Christian evangelist and pastor Dr. Tony Evans. The first show to turn me on to Christian radio programming. Dr. Evans's ministry, as well as *The Urban Alternative* radio show, can be accessed at www.tonyevans.org.

When God Doesn't Make Sense by Dr. James Dobson (Tyndale House, 1993) A practical book for those struggling with trials, heartaches, and tragedy. Many inspiring personal stories and a helpful question-and-answer format.

The Word in Life Study Bible (New King James Version) (Thomas Nelson, 1996) Clear, easy to read, and informative. Includes many articles dealing with the questions and issues raised in the scriptures and surrounding the biblical narrative, both historical and modern.

STUDY/DISCUSSION GUIDE

- Could you relate to where Bob was in his spiritual walk when Faith was born? How would you describe his faith at that time?

- Bob and Karen experienced a great deal of fear at Faith's birth. Have you ever been very fearful? What were the circumstances? What did you do to deal with that fear?

- Karen and Bob chose to go against the counsel of the neonatologist who advised them to hold the baby and "keep her warm as she passes on." What is your reaction to their decision?

- At one point, Bob reflected on how life is short—a "mist," a "vapor"—and actually took comfort in that thought. What led him to feel this way? Is this comforting to you? Why or why not?

- It has been said that medicine is more of an art than a science. Is there anything in this story that leads you to agree or disagree with this statement? How about from your own experience?

- Was community a part of Karen and Bob's experience with Faith? If so, how? Is community a part of your life? If so, how has it been valuable? Share an example.

- Bob and Karen believe that prayer made a difference in Faith's survival. Do you think prayers actually make a difference in situations like this? How? What makes you think this?

• Bob described Faith's survival and thriving as a miracle. Some people believe miracles happen today, some believe they used to but no longer occur, and some believe they have never occurred at all. What do you believe and why?

• In the NICU, some babies in Faith's situation did not do nearly as well as she did, and some even passed away, despite the same medical attention and deep spiritual belief on the part of their parents. What are your thoughts about this?

• After the events of this book, Bob described himself as having a "naïve faith." Jesus said, "Ye must be as little children to enter the kingdom of God." What do these statements mean to you?

• Karen and Bob said they believe that God saved Faith's life. Do you feel God works in your life? How? What makes you believe this?

• How did Bob and Karen's faith change after their daughter's birth? Has anything in your life ever radically changed your faith?